SPECTRUM™ 5

A Communicative Course in English

Sandra Costinett
with Donald R. H. Byrd

Donald R. H. Byrd *Project Director*

Anna Veltfort *Art Director*

Deborah Goldblatt *Developmental Editor*

PRENTICE HALL REGENTS, Englewood Cliffs, NJ 07632

Cover design: Garrett Loubé
Cover photo: © P. Beck, 1982. All rights reserved.
Design assistance: Lisa Schneck/Donna Eshleman
Mechanicals: Regents Production Department

SPECTRUM Textbook 5

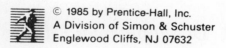

© 1985 by Prentice-Hall, Inc.
A Division of Simon & Schuster
Englewood Cliffs, NJ 07632

Printed in the United States of America

10 9 8 7 6

ISBN 0-13-826678-6 01

Prentice-Hall International (UK) Limited, *London*
Prentice-Hall of Australia Pty. Limited, *Sydney*
Prentice-Hall Canada Inc., *Toronto*
Prentice-Hall Hispanoamericana, S.A., *Mexico*
Prentice-Hall of India Private Limited, *New Delhi*
Prentice-Hall of Japan, Inc., *Tokyo*
Simon & Schuster Asia Pte. Ltd., *Singapore*
Editora Prentice-Hall do Brasil, Ltda., *Rio de Janeiro*

Authors

Donald R. H. Byrd *Project director*
Sandra Costinett *Textbook author*
Diane Warshawsky *Textbook author*
Nancy Frankfort *Teacher's edition author*
Joan Dye *Teacher's edition author*

David P. Rein *Workbook author*
Sharon Abrams *Workbook author*
Anna Veltfort *Art direction and page design*

Consultants

Mercedes Alvarez Lovell *Professor of English, Instituto Ramiro de Maeztu, Madrid, Spain*

Pedro I. Cohen *Professor of English, Linguistics, and Education, University of Panama*

Ikuo Koike *Professor of English and Linguistics, Keio University, Tokyo, Japan*

Nitza Lladó-Torres *Language Director, Basic Spanish, Department of Spanish and Portuguese, University of Southern California*

Ana María Payán Ramos *Director, English Teachers College, Escuela Normal Superior, Toluca, Edo. Mexico, Mexico*

Lucy Portela *ESL Bilingual Consultant, San Juan, Puerto Rico*

Barry P. Taylor *English Department, San Francisco State University*

Editorial staff

Deborah Goldblatt *Developmental and content editor*
John K. Cook *Project editor*
Kathy Niemczyk *Consulting editor*
Robert Sietsema *Photo editor*

Acknowledgments

Illustrations

Pages 2–3, 8–9 by Donna Eshleman; pages 4, 28, 68, 92, 110, 116 by Anne Burgess; pages 12, 15, 36, 39, 84 by Kimble Pendleton Mead; pages 16–17, 37, 40–41, 76, 88–89, 100 by Randy Jones; pages 18–19, 44, 86, 93, 108 by Keith Bendis; pages 52, 61, 95, 98, 103, 106, 112–113, 125 by Anna Veltfort; pages 56–57 by Eileen McKeating; page 58 by Nilda Gómez Scherer.

The engravings and collages on pages 32–33, 50, 82–83, 99, 124, and 126 were provided by Robert Sietsema.

Photo Credits

Pages 5, 32–33, 53: © Laimute E. Druskis; pages 8–9: J. Gerard Smith; pages 11, 24–25, 34–35, 43, 72–73, 121: Robert Sietsema; pages 20, 47, 81 *lower left:* © 1985 Donna Jernigan; page 26: Ron Riesterer/Oakland Tribune Photo; page 29: © Beryl Goldberg; page 31: R. Goldblatt Collection; pages 42, 49 *lower:* New York Daily News Photo; page 48: © Louisa Preston 1984; page 49 *upper left, upper right, middle,* 67 *top,* 80 *left,* 81 *top, upper right, lower right:* UPI/Bettmann Archive; page 63; © Geoffrey Hiller; pages 66, 67 *middle:* GTE; pages 74–75 *background,* 74 *inset:* Suzanne DeChillo/The New York Times; page 75 *inset:* © P. Grant; page 76: © Kit Kittle; page 80 *upper:* Milt Crossen/North American Soccer League, *lower:* Bridgeport Jai-Alai; page 90: Sara Krulwich/The New York Times; pages 96–97: Phototeque; page 107: Library of Congress; pages 114–115: NASA; page 122: © 1985 Bayard.

Realia

Pages 2–3, 10–11, 18–19, 26–27, 34–35, 42–43, 50–51, 66–67, 74–75, 82–83, 90–91, 98–99, 106–107, 114–115 by Anna Veltfort; pages 6 (bottom), 14, 22, 30, 46, 47, 58, 60, 62, 64, 70, 78, 109, 110, 117, 120–121, 122, 124, 126, 128 by Nilda Gómez Scherer.

Permissions

Pages 2–3: Susan H. Butcher; pages 10–11: Copyright © 1983 by The New York Times Company. Reprinted by permission; page 18: Peter Muller; page 26–27: Reprinted by permission of The Sterling Lord Agency Inc. Copyright © 1983 by Dick Schaap; pages 34–35: Reprinted from THE SOAP OPERA BOOK by Manuela Soares. Copyright © 1978 by Latham Publishing. Used by permission of Harmony Books, a division of Crown Publishers, Inc.; page 42: Copyright © 1977 by The New York Times Company. Reprinted by permission; pages 50–51: Roderick MacLeish; page 58: Copyright © 1984 by The New York Times Company. Reprinted by permission; page 60: Excerpted with permission of USA TODAY; page 62: Reprinted with permission of USA TODAY; page 64: Excerpted with permission of USA TODAY; page 66: WGBH–Boston, NOVA, © 1983, Addison-Wesley, Reading, Massachusetts, pp. 220–223. Reprinted with permission; pages 74–75: Copyright © 1983 by The New York Times Company. Reprinted by permission; page 82: Reprinted by permission of SPRING, Nov./Dec. 1983 Copyright Rodale Press, Inc. All rights reserved; page 90: Copyright © 1982 by The New York Times Company. Reprinted by permission; page 91: Reprinted with permission of United Press International, Inc.; page 98: Condensed from Paula Span, PEOPLE Weekly, February 21, © 1983, Time Inc.; pages 104–105: © World Copyright by Quino; page 106: LA Times–Washington Post Service; page 122: Copyright © 1984 by Newsweek, Inc. All rights reserved. Reprinted by permission; page 124: Reprinted with permission of USA TODAY; page 126: Reprinted with permission of United Press International, Inc.; page 128: Reprinted with permission of the *New York Daily News.*

Source notes

page 114: Eugene F. Kranz, "Space Travel," *The World Book Encyclopedia,* 1984, XVIII, 568b, 572b–f; Natalie Angier, "Welcome to the Cosmic Hotel," *Discover,* April 1984, pp. 24–27; Arthur Myers, "Space Cities," in *EDL Reading Power Module,* eds. Helen Frackenpohl Morris et al., (New York: McGraw-Hill, Inc., 1979), G-Science Selections, pp. 18-19.

Contents: *scope and sequence*

v

Introduction

SPECTRUM is a complete, six-level course in English as a second/foreign language. It is aimed at adults and young adults in secondary schools, universities, and centers for adult education, both in the United States and abroad. SPECTRUM 1 and SPECTRUM 2 are for beginning students. SPECTRUM 1 can be used in classes of zero-level beginners. SPECTRUM 2 reviews and expands all the basic material in SPECTRUM 1 and thus is useful for teaching "false beginners." SPECTRUM 3 and 4 are for intermediate students and SPECTRUM 5 and 6 for advanced students. Each of the six levels has a fully illustrated textbook with an accompanying teacher's edition, a workbook, and an audio program recorded on cassettes.

SPECTRUM has three basic aims: (1) to provide motivating materials that teach students to function in real-life situations in which English is spoken, (2) to teach only authentic English, and (3) to give students a feeling of success and achievement in language learning.

THE COMMUNICATIVE APPROACH TO LANGUAGE TEACHING

SPECTRUM is based on the communicative approach to language teaching. The series teaches basic linguistic functions such as *asking for information, talking about feelings, making suggestions,* and *apologizing.* Students learn language that can be put to immediate use in both speaking and writing. They also learn appropriate language for different situations, such as the formal speech used with strangers and informal speech used with friends. Exercises practice the basic functions and structures. They encourage students to give personal information and express their own ideas and feelings. Natural conversation is stimulated in the classroom.

SPECTRUM recognizes that students can understand more English than they are able to use. This basic distinction between *receptive* and *productive* language allows new language to be systematically introduced before it is practiced. Students need only understand receptive language, which is tested in *right/wrong, multiple choice,* and *matching* exercises. Much of the receptive language becomes productive in later units or levels. Students then actively practice the familiar functions and structures through more challenging *role-playing* and *writing* exercises.

Grammar is carefully graded throughout the series. However, more difficult structures may be introduced *formulaically* when they are needed to perform a given function appropriately. In level 1, students learn expressions such as *Could you spell your last name?* and *May I take a message?*, although the modal auxiliaries *could* and *may* are not analyzed systematically until the intermediate level. In the advanced level, the same structures are expanded further, as students learn to form passive sentences containing modal auxiliaries. This system of *preview-review* works as follows:

- Preview: structures are introduced formulaically.
- Analysis: structures are examined and practiced systematically.
- Review: structures are recycled for further practice.

Useful *formulas*, such as *How do you do* and *Nice meeting you* are also taught in SPECTRUM, without analyzing their structure.

THE TEXTBOOK

There are sixteen units in the textbook, two of which are review. Each of the other fourteen units contains eight pages and is divided into four major sections: (1) Reading—first and second pages; (2) *Try this* (warm-up) and conversation—third page; (3) *Ways to say it* (functions and grammar)—fourth, fifth, and sixth pages; and (4) *Your turn* (free conversation activity), *Listen in* (listening), and *On your own* (writing)—seventh and eighth pages.

A 500-word *Reading* selection establishes the theme of the unit. Students read authentic newspaper or magazine articles that have been carefully adapted for use in SPECTRUM. The articles are accompanied by a variety of pre-reading, as-you-read, and follow-up activities that develop reading skills.

The *Try this* section is an oral activity in which students use grammar, functions, or vocabulary they have studied in previous levels or units. Students may role-play a situation, discuss a topic, or talk about personal experiences. The activity is intended not only to review familiar language but also to motivate students to learn more sophisticated ways of performing a function or discussing a topic. The conversation that follows presents new language students can use to do this. The conversation is first presented receptively. Students then test their understanding of the new functions and grammar through one or more receptive *Figure it out* exercises.

Students then move from reception to production on the *Ways to say it* pages. Communicative activities, which teach new language from the conversation, allow students to role-play situations, exchange personal information, and give opinions. Each unit focuses on one function or a group of related functions, and students are taught alternate ways to perform the same function. When appropriate, writing activities are also included. *Close-up* or grammar exercises follow selected activities and enable students to practice the structures introduced in the unit as they appear. Exercises are contextualized and natural language is used.

The *Your turn* pages integrate free conversation, listening (*Listen in*), and writing (*On your own*) in a series of thematically related activities. A variety of photos, artwork, or short articles suggest different topics for discussion and writing. Working in small groups, students draw on their personal experiences and perform a wide number of functions. Students not only practice the new language in the unit but are free to use any of the language learned so far.

THE TEACHER'S EDITION

The teacher's edition of the textbook gives step-by-step instructions for all exercises; suggestions for additional activities; answer keys; the script for all *Listen in* activities; and cultural, usage, and pronunciation notes. An answer key for workbook exercises and the scripts for workbook listening activities are also included.

A *Purpose* page begins every unit of the teacher's edition. It states the objectives of the unit and lists the functions and forms that are taught. It also presents suggestions for lesson plans.

THE WORKBOOK

Each unit of the workbook reinforces the functions, structures, and vocabulary taught in the corresponding textbook unit. Familiar material is presented in new contexts. The workbook focuses on developing reading, writing, and listening skills.

THE AUDIO PROGRAM

The audio program records the conversation that presents the new material in each textbook unit and the *Listen in* activities. In addition, all listening activities in the workbook are recorded. All dialogues on the audio program have been recorded at normal conversational speed, and feature authentic-sounding voices and sound effects. A cassette symbol appears next to each section of the textbook and workbook which is recorded.

ONE WOMAN'S RACE ACROSS ALASKA

by Susan Butcher

Although Susan Butcher was born in Cambridge, Massachusetts, her love of the outdoors and dogs took her to Alaska in 1975. After three years of building and training a team of dogs, she entered the Iditarod—a 1,000-mile dog-sled race from Anchorage to Nome. She finished nineteenth, then ninth in 1979, and fifth in 1980 and 1981. In 1982, she was determined to win.

Tekla, my most experienced dog, is limping, too tired to go on. I know she has reached her limit. Tears roll down my cheeks. She, who led my team all the way in my first three Iditarods, who has saved my life more than once, who can even read my mind, now has to be left behind.

A wrong turn in a heavy snowstorm the first day of the race has taken me 20 miles out of my way. The four hours lost in getting back on the trail have put me far behind the front-runners.

With only 11 of my original 15 dogs left, I start out again for Nome, still 938 miles away. In these first two days on the trail, I have had only four hours of sleep.

After a 24-hour rest at Rohn and four hot meals, my determination to stay in the race is stronger than ever. The falling snow grows heavier, completely covering the trail, but I keep going. I catch up with the leaders, who have lost their way and are waiting for daylight. For four and a half days and 353 miles, we take turns breaking the trail through the deep snow.

At the village of Ruby, the weather improves—but only temporarily. The sky is clear, but the temperature drops to 45 degrees below zero as I start out alone down the frozen Yukon River. If I stay too long on the sled, I risk serious frostbite. Jogging too long behind it can damage my lungs. So I alternate between running and riding.

A raging storm moves in, burying the trail. Those of us in the lead must work together again to break the trail. After 50 miles, we find shelter for the night.

Another day's travel brings us to Unalakleet. The weather worsens. Winds rise to 60 miles an hour. Visi-

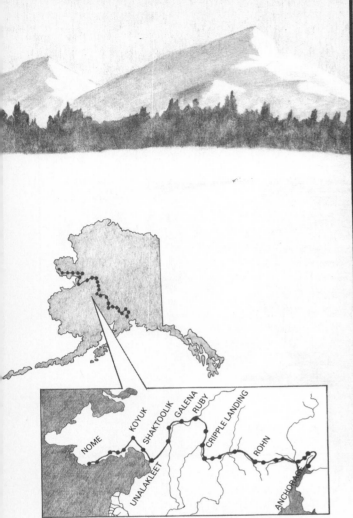

Map shows route of race. Dots show checkpoints.

bility drops to near zero. My eyelashes freeze shut and so do the eyelashes of my dogs. I stop often to clear their eyes and check their feet.

I reach Shaktoolik late that night with a frostbitten face. When I awaken the next morning, the winds are gusting up to 80 miles an hour, and the snowdrifts are 30 feet high. I wait 52 hours in the village before the storm lets up.

Only 231 miles to go, but all of them difficult. We push through the continuing storm. Seven lead teams are traveling close together. Another dog on my team must drop out, and I have just nine dogs left.

Thirty miles to go. I am in fifth place behind Rick Swenson, Jerry Austin, Emmitt Peters, and Ernie Baumgartner. The final push is on.

I pass Ernie and pull away. I pass Emmitt, but he stays right behind me. Only 22 miles now. "Go! Go! Go!" I shout to my dogs. I soon outdistance Emmitt and pass Jerry. My hopes brighten. But there's still Rick, barely visible in the distance. He beats us into Nome by 3 minutes and 43 seconds. The race has lasted 16 days.

Now I have only one dream to go: to be Number One.

Figure it out

1. **Before starting to read, look at the artwork and the title of the article. What do you think the article is about? Does your answer change after you have read the first paragraph?**

2. **As you read, try to figure out the answers to the questions below. Do not stop to look up new words until you have finished the article. Then adjust your answers if necessary.**
   1. What exactly is a dog-sled race? How would you describe one to somebody?
   2. What is difficult about a dog-sled race?
   3. What is Susan Butcher like? What clues does the article give about her personality?

3. **Put these sentences in the correct order. Then use them and any other information you need to summarize the story briefly in your own words. Make sure to say whether or not Susan Butcher won the race.**
   _____ 1. The weather worsened with higher winds and poor visibility.
   _____ 2. Butcher arrived in Nome a few minutes behind Rick Swenson.
   _____ 3. Butcher went 20 miles out of her way.
   _____ 4. Butcher was in fifth place.
   _____ 5. Butcher caught up with the leaders, and they took turns breaking the trail.
   _____ 6. Butcher left behind her most experienced dog.

4. **The suffix -en in worsen means "to become worse." In frighten, it means "to make someone become afraid." Complete the paragraph with appropriate verbs from the list, making sure to put them in their correct form.**

   awaken   frighten   sharpen
   blacken   lessen   worsen
   brighten   redden

   I _____ early. The sky is slowly _____ , but the temperature has dropped. I step outside and my face _____ from the wind. The weather is very bad, but it doesn't _____ me. I know the finish line is near. Nothing can _____ my determination to win.

3

You made it!

Try this

The 10-kilometer "Run for Your Life" marathon, held every year to raise money for heart disease research, is about to begin. You are a reporter covering the event, and your partner is one of the runners. Interview him or her, using the expressions *How long . . . ?*, *ever*, and *before this.*

A TV reporter is interviewing Liz Joseph, who just finished last in the "Run for Your Life" marathon.

- Reporter
- ○ Liz Joseph

● You made it!
○ Yeah!
● How does it feel?
○ Great! I mean, it's not everyone who comes in last.
● You look pretty tired.
○ I am, but I'm so excited I don't think I'll be able to get to sleep for a while.
● Was this your first race?
○ Yes. I've only been running for two months. When I signed up, I'd only been running for two weeks! Everyone said it was too soon to enter a race.
● Well, you certainly showed them! Was there ever a time when you thought you would drop out?

○ Well, it was such a hot day that I started feeling a little tired pretty early. And I hadn't even gone three miles when I got a pain in my side.
● How was that last big hill?
○ Oh, that was a killer. I'd just made it about halfway when my right knee started giving me trouble. I didn't know if I had enough energy to get to the top. But I managed to do it.
● What made you decide to enter the race?
○ Well, I'd always wanted to see if I could make it through a race like this. Besides, I knew they'd give me one of those cute T-shirts.

Figure it out

Fill in the blanks with *I've*, *I'd*, *I haven't*, or *I hadn't*.

1. _____ been running for two months and I really enjoy it.
2. _____ been running for two weeks when I entered the race.
3. _____ even run three miles and I'm already tired.
4. _____ even run three miles when I got a pain in my side.
5. _____ always wanted to run in a race, but I just never have.
6. _____ always wanted to run in a race until I sprained my ankle.

Ways to say it

1 **TALK ABOUT A DECISION**

Interview another student. Ask questions about your partner's life, past and present. Find out about a decision your partner has made and the situation that led up to it.

What made you decide to go into medicine?

Well, I'd always wanted to be a doctor, even as a small child. My mother was a doctor, and so was my grandfather. . . .

What made you decide to drive a truck?

I'd just finished high school and I needed a job. And I'd never been anywhere outside my hometown. . . .

What made you decide to change careers?

I'd been working at the same job for fifteen years, and one day I just woke up and said, "Enough!"

You *go into* a profession, *major in* a school subject, and *take up* a sport or leisure activity.

What made you decide to . . . ?	Well . . .
go into business for yourself major in mathematics move to the city take up running	I'd always heard . . . I'd just taken a course . . . I'd lived in a small town since . . . I'd been thinking about it for . . .

---

2 **Close-up**   PAST PERFECT

Affirmative and negative statements

I You He She We They	had ('d)	wanted	to be in a race.
		been	in a race before.
	hadn't	run	three miles when Jane hurt her knee.

had ▶ 'd
had not ▶ hadn't
I'd = I had *or* I would

past participle

Notice how past perfect questions are formed:

Had you ever been in a race before?
Hadn't you finished school when you got this job?

Notice how the past perfect continuous is formed:

How long had you been studying English when you went to London?
I'd been taking English in school for ten years.

Simple past and present perfect vs. past perfect

Use the simple past or present perfect to refer to a situation or event in the past:
    I got my first job in 1985. (a specified time in the past)
    I've already finished school. (at an unspecified time in the past)
	Use the past perfect to emphasize that one event in the past occurred before another:
	    I'd already finished school when I got my first job.
	    (First, I finished school. Then I got the job.)

Use the present perfect to refer to something that began in the past and continues into the present:
    I've always enjoyed running.
	Use the past perfect to refer to something that began in the past and continued until another point in the past:
	    I'd always enjoyed running until I entered my first race.

3 TELL A STORY

Write an article about Susan Butcher. Using the past perfect, describe the events that took place before the 1982 dog-sled race. Include the information in your notes on the right.

Start like this:

Susan Butcher and her dogs were waiting nervously for the 1982 Iditarod dog-sled race to begin. The month before the race she had put together . . .

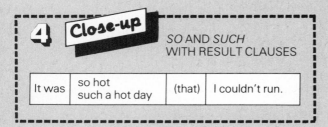

- The month before the race she put together 1,500 pounds of food and equipment and left it at 24 checkpoints along the 1,000-mile course.
- Her preparations began soon after the 1981 race.
- In that race and in 1980, her sled was the fifth one to cross the finish line.
- The year before, she came in ninth.
- In her first Iditarod dog-sled race in 1978, she finished nineteenth.
- She trained a team of dogs for three years for this first race.
- She first came to Alaska in 1975 to meet this challenge.

4 Close-up   *SO* AND *SUCH* WITH RESULT CLAUSES

| It was | so hot
such a hot day | (that) | I couldn't run. |

5 EMPHASIZE SOMETHING

Learn some interesting facts by reading the "Strange But True" column. Then share what you've read with another student. Include a sentence with *so* or *such* in each conversation.

- Hmm . . . I didn't know this. There's a disease that's called laughing sickness.
- Oh, come on now! I find that hard to believe.
- No, really. It's so rare that it only affects one tribe in New Guinea.
- Wait, now that you mention it, I think I read about that somewhere.

Strange But True

It's hard to imagine not liking to laugh. But for certain people, the victims of laughing sickness, laughing is no fun. This rare disease only affects one tribe in New Guinea.

The largest cake in the world was baked in Baltimore, Maryland, in 1976. The cake weighed 31,755 kilograms (69,860 pounds), and it took 120,000 eggs to make it.

The highest temperature ever recorded was in Libya. The temperature once reached 58°C (136.4°F), even in the shade.

What is black and white and cute and cuddly? If you answered "a panda," you're wrong. Except for the kind in toy stores, pandas aren't cuddly at all. They're very bad-tempered animals. Even zookeepers are extremely careful around them.

Some ways to start
Hmm . . . I didn't know this. Listen to this. Did you know that . . . ? I was just reading that . . .

Some reactions
Oh, come on now! I find that hard to believe. Yes, I've heard that. No kidding! That's interesting. Now that you mention it, I think I read about that.

6 **Close-up**   *TOO* AND *NOT . . . ENOUGH* WITH INFINITIVES

It's	too hot	to	run.
He doesn't run	fast enough		win.

◄ *too* + adjective or adverb
adjective or adverb + *enough*

There were	too many people		see anything.
It takes	too much time	to	walk there.
I don't have	enough energy		run.

◄ *too many* + count noun
too much + mass noun
enough + count or mass noun

7 GIVE A REACTION

In the conversations below, restate the second speaker's reaction so that it includes either *too* or *not . . . enough*, and an infinitive.

1. ● I think I'll enter the "Run for Your Life" race.
   ○ But you've only been running for two weeks!
   But you haven't been running long enough to enter a race!

2. ● Janet and I would like to get married.
   ○ But you're only seventeen years old!

3. ● How did you do on the test?
   ○ Not too well. There were a lot of essay questions that we had to answer.

4. ● Let's get a bite to eat before the play.
   ○ It's already after seven. The play starts at eight.

5. ● What did you think of the new Kurasawa movie?
   ○ We were sitting so far back that we couldn't read the subtitles.

6. ● How was the lecture?
   ○ I was so exhausted after work that I couldn't even pay attention.

8 TELL ABOUT A PAST EXPERIENCE

Write a paragraph about a personal experience that was frustrating, disappointing, or difficult in some way. Explain why, and then tell about the situation that led up to the experience. When you have finished, share your experience with another student.

Some topics	
an exam	your driving test
a class	a job interview
a social situation	a contest or competition

Last summer, I went to the United States to study English. After I registered in the program, I had to take a placement exam. I had just arrived in the United States the day before, and I was so tired I couldn't keep my eyes open. I hadn't studied much English yet, and I didn't know enough English to understand a lot of the questions.

Your turn

1.

It's 6:00 in the evening and you are riding the train. There are many different kinds of people on the train with you, and as you look at them, you wonder how they spent their day and what their lives have been like. Look at the people in the photos, and then work in groups to make up stories about some of them. Consider each of these questions:

1. Where is the person going and what had the person been doing before he or she got on the train? Are there any clues in the photo?
2. What sort of lifestyle does the person have? What made him or her decide to choose this lifestyle?
3. Has the person made a big decision recently? If so, what led up to it?
4. Has something exciting, interesting, important, disappointing, or sad happened to the person recently? If so, what led up to the event or situation?

2. Listen in ▭

Read the statements below. Then listen to two conversations taking place on the train and say *Right* or *Wrong*. Correct the wrong statements.

Conversation 1
1. Nancy got a job.
2. The company didn't interview anyone but Nancy.

Conversation 2
3. Bill decided to change colleges.
4. Bill had discussed his plans with his parents before he made a decision.

3. On your own

Your local newspaper has a weekly column called "Slice of Life." In it, the paper prints interesting stories about people. Write a story for the column about someone on the train. You may write one of the stories your group made up or write about someone else. You may even wish to write about yourself.

FINGERS, CHOPSTICKS, OR FORKS

by **Bryce Nelson**

① All the world is divided into three parts—finger-feeders, chopstick-feeders, and fork-feeders. Why people fall into these categories, however, is a mystery.

② Fork-feeders are most numerous in Europe, North America, and Latin America; chopstick-feeders in most of eastern Asia; and finger-feeders in much of Africa, the Middle East, Indonesia, and India. This means that fork-feeders are outnumbered two to one.

③ Fork-users have historically been in the minority. People have eaten with their fingers for most of human existence. As little as three centuries ago, most Western Europeans still used their fingers. French historian Fernand Braudel tells of a preacher in Germany who lived during the Middle Ages. The preacher thought the fork was evil and called it a "diabolical luxury; God would not have given us fingers if he had wished us to use such an instrument."

④ Forks and chopsticks won favor because they made it easier to handle hot food. Before these instruments, people usually ate hot food with a piece of flat bread. The exception was in China, where flat bread was probably not eaten.

⑤ According to Dr. K. C. Chang of Harvard University, Chinese food was served in small portions which did not require cutting with a knife or fork. There was, however, a need for food to be carried from the bowl to the mouth, and chopsticks came along to meet that need. Some of the oldest Chinese chopsticks date from 1200 B.C.

⑥ The fork made its way to Western tables several hundred years later, but it was not immediately accepted. Forks were used for many years in Europe and the Near East, but only as kitchen implements. The general use of forks as eating utensils started with the Byzantines in the tenth century A.D. (The Byzantine Empire extended through southeast Europe, southwest Asia, and northern Africa, including what is now Greece and parts of Turkey, Italy, and Egypt.) The first illustration of their use at meals was in a manuscript from the monastery of Montecassino in Italy in 1022 A.D.

⑦ Although the fork entered society on the tables of the rich and well-born, many members of royalty, including Elizabeth I of England and Louis XIV of France, ate with their fingers. When Napoleon III of France, a

Figure it out

1. **Before you read the article, try to guess the answers to the questions below. When you have finished reading, correct your answers.**

   1. People around the world eat with their hands, chopsticks, or forks. Where is each way most popular?
   2. When and why were chopsticks and forks invented?
   3. How have people's attitudes toward the three ways of eating changed over time?

2. **As you read, try to figure out the main idea of each paragraph. When you have finished reading, choose *a* or *b*. for the paragraphs below.**

   1. Paragraph 3:
      a. Throughout most of history, people have eaten with their fingers.
      b. Some people used to think the fork was evil.

   2. Paragraph 7:
      a. Sailors in the British Navy ate with their fingers.
      b. Until fairly recently, the fork was not completely accepted in Europe.

   3. Paragraph 8:
      a. There is new ethnic pride among non-Westerners
      b. Finger-feeding is starting to be more popular.

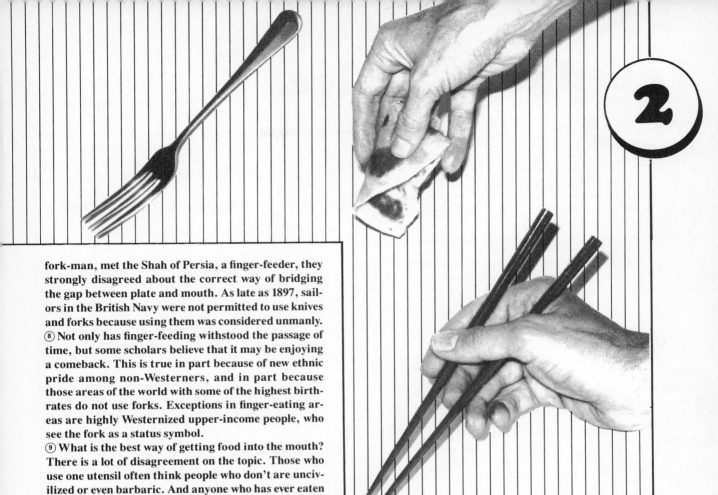

fork-man, met the Shah of Persia, a finger-feeder, they strongly disagreed about the correct way of bridging the gap between plate and mouth. As late as 1897, sailors in the British Navy were not permitted to use knives and forks because using them was considered unmanly. ⑧ Not only has finger-feeding withstood the passage of time, but some scholars believe that it may be enjoying a comeback. This is true in part because of new ethnic pride among non-Westerners, and in part because those areas of the world with some of the highest birthrates do not use forks. Exceptions in finger-eating areas are highly Westernized upper-income people, who see the fork as a status symbol.

⑨ What is the best way of getting food into the mouth? There is a lot of disagreement on the topic. Those who use one utensil often think people who don't are uncivilized or even barbaric. And anyone who has ever eaten at a formal table elaborately set with many different kinds of knives, spoons, and forks can sympathize with Oscar Wilde, who said, "The world was my oyster, but I used the wrong fork."

3. The prefix *out-* can be put before a verb to mean "to do something more than, better than, or longer than." Complete each sentence, choosing the appropriate verb below. Make sure to use the correct form of the verb.

outdistance   outgrow   outlive   outnumber   outweigh (be more important than)

1. In the last 30 miles, Susan Butcher _____ three racers and finished second.
2. Unless I start taking better care of my health, my parents might _____ me.
3. Finger-feeders _____ fork-feeders two to one.
4. My children _____ their clothes so fast that I have to buy new clothes every month.
5. When someone is trying to make a good impression, table manners can _____ conversation and personality.

I need your advice.

You are invited to a formal dinner, and you want to make a good impression. Ask another student for advice on what to do and what not to do.

The Santanas are having dinner at the Colemans' house. Victor Santana notices two sets of chopsticks on the table.

● Victor Santana
○ Bob Coleman
▲ Ann Coleman
△ Elena Santana

● Low on forks? I would have been happy to bring some.
○ No, no, we're just practicing our chopstick technique.
▲ A Japanese couple is having us over for dinner next week.
○ One thing I'll say for these things is I don't eat as much. It's too hard to get the food to my mouth.
▲ Especially those little grains of rice. I had to practice long and hard to manage those.
△ Bringing the bowl to your mouth makes it easier. In fact, it seems to me I read somewhere that it's considered very rude not to.
▲ It's so easy to offend people when you don't know their customs. I remember one time a friend of mine from Switzerland had us over for dinner. I baked a cake for dessert. Later I found out you're not supposed to take your host any food.
△ They must have thought you were terribly rude.
▲ I'm sure they did, but they were too polite to say anything.
○ Listen, I need your advice. Do you think we should take our Japanese friends something?
△ Well, I wouldn't suggest taking food.... You could take something for their kids.
○ Good idea....Are we supposed to bow, do you think?
● Now wait . . . we *are* in the United States....
△ I don't think you have to bow. But remember, you must take off your shoes.
● And you mustn't wear socks with holes in them.
▲ Now there's some good advice!

Figure it out

Match.

1. I wouldn't suggest baking a cake.
2. Do you think we should bake a cake?
3. They must have baked a cake.
4. You could bake a cake.
5. You must bake a cake.

a. ask for advice
b. give advice
c. state an obligation
d. reach a conclusion

Ways to say it

1 ASK FOR AND GIVE ADVICE

Ask another student for practical advice. He or she will offer a suggestion.

- Uh, do you have a minute? I need your advice on something.
- ○ Sure. What can I help you with?
- Some friends of mine are coming to town for the weekend, and I don't have any idea where to take them.
- ○ I'd suggest going to the fair in Sevilla.
- That's a good idea. I hadn't thought of that.

Some topics
where to take an out-of-town guest
what to wear somewhere
what to make for an important dinner
buying something
how to get information about something
how to get out of a commitment (something you've told someone you'd do)

Some ways to ask for advice
I need your advice.
Do you think I should . . . ?
Am I supposed to . . . ?
I can't decide if I should . . .
I don't have any idea . . .
If you were me, would you . . . ? (informal)

Some ways to give advice
I'd (I wouldn't) suggest . . .
Why don't you . . . ?
How about . . . ?
Have you tried . . . ?
You could . . .
If I were you, I'd . . .

◄ The expressions *I'd suggest . . .*, *How about . . . ?*, and *Have you tried . . . ?* are followed by gerunds.

2 GIVE ADVICE

Complete the sentences with gerunds (verb + *ing*). Another student will give you advice on your problem.

- Speaking in front of people really makes me nervous.
- ○ If you practiced more, you'd probably get used to it. I'd suggest signing up for a course in public speaking.

1. _____ makes me nervous.
2. _____ is something I find difficult.
3. _____ is something I've never enjoyed doing.
4. _____ is something I don't think I'll ever be able to do.

3 TALK ABOUT CUSTOMS

Using the information in the box, tell another student about a time when you did something culturally inappropriate.

- It's so easy to offend people when you don't know their customs. I remember one time _____ . Later I found out _____ .
- ○ _____ must have _____ .

Some customs
In Switzerland, it's considered impolite to take food with you to a dinner.
In Japan, you should never leave your rice bowl on the table while you eat.
In Lebanon, you're not supposed to show that you're hungry when you go to someone's home for dinner.
In the United States, you should always ask your host before you take a friend along to dinner.

4 Close-up

GERUND VS. *IT* AS SUBJECT

Subject

Speaking in public	makes me nervous.	
It	makes me nervous	to speak in public.

5 **Rewrite the advertisement, changing the parts in brackets as in the example.**

Making a good impression is important. It's our business . . .

J. Alexander Career Institute
Training Courses and Seminars for the Career Person

[It's important to make a good impression.] [Helping you do just that is our business.]

We realize that [going on a big job interview can be frightening.] [Knowing how to behave is essential,] but [it's easier than you think to present yourself well.] Of course you need the basic skills to get the job you want, but beyond those, we've found that:

- [It's important to write a good résumé.]
- [It's essential to learn to express yourself with confidence.]
- [It's vital to look like the right person for the job.]

We will show you how to do all this and more. Remember, [it can be the beginning of a bright new future to take a course at J. Alexander Career Institute.] Register now, and look forward to success.

6 (TALK ABOUT SOCIAL RULES)

Discuss some of the rules of social behavior in your country. If you're familiar with other cultures, make comparisons. Use the expressions in the box.

 A friend just told me that you must always give taxi drivers a tip. I didn't know that.
○ Yes, you're supposed to because they depend on the money. Tips are a big part of their salary.
● What about maids in hotels? Do you have to tip them?
○ Well, you should unless the tip is on your bill.
● But what if more than one person has cleaned your room? . . .

Some topics	Some expressions
giving and receiving tips, gifts, or compliments arriving on time invitations and table manners shaking hands, kissing, bowing use of first names and titles (Mr., Mrs., etc.) special language to use with people of different ages and statuses	You must . . . You mustn't . . . You have to . . . You don't have to . . . You're not supposed to, but . . . Do you have to . . . ? Is it O.K. if . . . ?

◄ Use *must* to express a strong obligation and *mustn't* to express a strong prohibition.

14

7 　　　*MUST* AND *MUSTN'T*: OBLIGATION AND PROHIBITION

Affirmative statements

I You	must	go now. be on time.

Negative statements

We You	mustn't	be late for dinner. wear shoes in the house.

▲

(must not ▶ mustn't)

Must vs. *have to*

Use *must* to express a strong obligation: I *must* finish the report tomorrow. (It's extremely important.)	Also use *have to* to express a strong obligation, although it is a little less forceful than *must*: I *have to* meet Jim at seven. (I don't want to be late.)
Use the negative of *must* to express a prohibition: We *mustn't* call Susan so early. (We might wake her up.)	Use the negative of *have to* when there is no obligation: We *don't have to* call Susan so early. (She'll be home later.)
Use *must* in official correspondence: We *must* receive your application by June 1.	

Must: obligation and prohibition vs. logical conclusion

Obligation and prohibition

Logical conclusion

Use the contraction *mustn't*: We *mustn't* bother Joe. He's not feeling well.	Do not use the contraction: The restaurant is dark. It *must not* be open.
Use *had to* for the past form: I *had to* practice every evening for the concert.	Use *must have* for the past form: You played so well. You *must have* practiced a lot.

8 **Complete each sentence with an affirmative or negative form of *must* or *have to* and a form of the verb in parentheses. Make sure to use the correct tense.**

1. I _____ any later than five because Paulo is coming over at six. (leave)
2. Kay got home late because she _____ the bus. Her car broke down. (take)
3. You _____ between eight and nine because I was home the rest of the evening. (call)
4. Dan _____ who I am because he hasn't said hello. (remember)
5. The Ramones _____ to meet us because they're always on time. (forget)
6. Charlie _____ his trip to London because he couldn't get a passport in time. He was so disappointed. (cancel)
7. I _____ late last night because I finished all my work early. (work)
8. We _____ to talk quietly because Sarah is sleeping. (try)

Your turn

1.

What advice would you give to each of these people? Discuss each situation in groups.

2. Listen in 🔊

Read the statement below. Then listen to the conversation between Tim Cooper and Jane Molina, another teacher, and choose *a, b,* or *c.*

Jane thinks Tim should _____ .
a. take the boy to a doctor
b. get in touch with the boy's parents
c. talk to the principal

3.

Would you give different advice to Tim Cooper, based on his conversation with Jane? Discuss this question in groups.

4. On your own

Write a letter, choosing one of the topics below.

1. Imagine that you've met Joan Chasen. Write to her, giving her advice.
2. Imagine that you're a relative of Richard Diego's. Write to him, giving him advice.
3. Write to a friend of yours, asking for advice about a real problem that you have.

Joan Chasen, a teenager from Chicago, is going to spend the summer in your city or country. She's never been there before, and she isn't very familiar with your customs.

Tim Cooper is a kindergarten teacher. One of the children in his class doesn't look healthy and often gets sick. Tim recently noticed that the little boy's lunch bag usually has only candy or cake in it.

Richard Diego just started a job at a large company. Richard used to have his own business, but he recently sold it. He's very independent and likes to make his own decisions. He's never worked in an office before.

Laurie Smith is having dinner with some friends of her parents, and everyone is discussing politics. Laurie strongly disagrees with the others' opinions and is becoming very angry as she listens to them.

Susan Green is a chemist and she loves her job. The work is interesting and she's well paid. However, she's overworked because her boss doesn't work very hard. He takes long coffee breaks and reads the newspaper.

Mark Seda's cousin died on Friday. Mark has an important job interview the same day as the funeral. He didn't know his cousin well.

PETS
as status symbols

by
Peter Muller

Londoners who happened to walk along the Thames during the mid-thirteenth century might have seen a large white bear walking down to the river. Following behind would be a man, holding the bear with a long leash. The man would sit on the riverbank while the bear, still attached to the leash, would go into the water and fish for its dinner.

The bear belonged to King Henry III. Henry wanted to save money, so he had the bear catch its own food. The people of London must have appreciated his sense of economy since they paid for the bear's expenses.

Henry was not the first king to keep large pets. In fact, practically every royal head of state from the beginning of civilization to the French Revolution seemed to want to own animals of great beauty — animals that were the biggest, the strangest, or the most dangerous.

Both the ancient Egyptians and Chinese collected animals for pleasure. Chinese emperors kept them in places called "parks of intelligence," while Egyptian royalty kept monkeys, leopards, and occasionally a giraffe on the palace grounds.

Birds, exotic and familiar, were popular in Rome. When Octavian, later the Emperor Augustus, defeated Marc Antony in battle, he was supposedly given a raven trained to say *Ave, Caesar victor imperator*, "Hail, Caesar, victorious leader." Octavian was very pleased until he learned that the trainer had taught another raven to say *Ave, victor imperator Antoni*, in case Antony had won.

Snakes were so popular in Rome at one time that they became a nuisance in the city. Sometimes during banquets, they would glide over the tables and among the guests who were eating. Dangerous animals were tamed and then permitted to walk freely through the houses of the rich. The Emperor Elagabalus had lions and leopards that entered the dining room and even the bedrooms of guests.

As trade routes to Africa and Asia began to open up, every aristocrat wanted to have exotic animals. Louis IX of France had an elephant and a porcupine, Charles V of Spain had seven seals, and Henry IV of France had four monkeys and a parrot.

Charles V of France loved birds and kept every room at Vincennes, where he grew up, filled with them. He put them in cages made of gold and silver.

Not only did rich people keep pets, they made them do strange things for their entertainment. Napoleon's wife Josephine had an orangutan that sat at her dinner table in a coat. A Portuguese princess went to the trouble of getting zebras because she thought they would look pretty pulling the royal children in a little carriage. To her great disappointment, she got no cooperation from the zebras.

What a way to save money!

Owning and displaying exotic pets has continued into more modern times. It is said that the French poet Baudelaire walked a lobster on a leash, and Jack Johnson, the American prizefighter, took his leopard for walks through the streets of Paris. But over the years, it has become obvious that the care of exotic animals requires specialized knowledge. Generally speaking, the feeling of both the public and the experts goes against keeping bears in the backyard or lions in the living room.

Figure it out

1. **A status symbol is something a person has or displays so other people will think he or she is important. As you read, think about whether "Pets as Status Symbols" is a good title for the article. When you have finished, give reasons why or why not.**

2. **As you read the article, try to figure out what its main themes are. Then say *Theme* or *Supporting Fact* for each statement below. For each supporting fact, tell which theme(s) it supports.**

   1. Almost every king and queen until the French Revolution kept strange pets.
   2. Henry III had a bear that he used to take down to the Thames so it could fish for its food.
   3. The rich kept strange pets not only as status symbols but also for pleasure and entertainment.
   4. People still own exotic pets, but, in general, the public feels very differently about this now.
   5. Napoleon's wife Josephine had an orangutan that sat at her dinner table in a coat.

3. **Match each highlighted pronoun in the next to last paragraph with a word or expression it refers to. The pronouns are listed in the order in which they appear.**

1. they	a. the zebras
2. them	b. the pets
3. their	c. the rich people('s)
4. her	d. the Portuguese princess('s)
5. she	e. Josephine's
6. they	
7. her	
8. she	

4. **The suffix *-tion* changes a verb into a noun, as in *civilize* and *civilization*. Fill in each blank with an appropriate noun from the list.**

appreciation	graduation	revolution
civilization	permission	transportation
cooperation	reservation	

   1. When a Portuguese princess tried to have zebras pull her children in a carriage, she got no _____ from the zebras.
   2. The French _____ took place in 1789.
   3. I'm looking forward to my college _____ .
   4. At many restaurants you need a _____ for dinner.
   5. I helped a friend with a report, and she took me out to dinner to express her _____ .

Oh, come on, Dad!

Try this

Discuss the advantages and disadvantages of having house pets. What kinds of animals make good pets? What kind of home is best for pets? What are some of the reasons people get pets?

Ten-year-old David Sinclair is trying to talk his parents into taking in a friend's dog. 📼

● Betty Sinclair	▲ David Sinclair
○ Paul Sinclair	△ Amy Sinclair

● Ted's leaving for Spain in two weeks and he still hasn't found anyone to take care of Ralph.

○ That doesn't surprise me. The dog has a miserable personality.

▲ Why don't we keep Ralph here?

● Oh, honey, I don't think Ralph is what we need right now. In any case, the landlord probably wouldn't let us keep him. He's afraid of dogs.

▲ True, but Ralph's just a little dog.

○ That's the worst kind. What's more, with our luck, the dog would bite him and he'd make us move out.

▲ Please, I'll take care of him. It'll be fun.

△ I could help David walk him.

○ Do you kids realize how much work a dog is?

● You know, it might be good for them, Paul. It would teach them responsibility.

○ That's asking a lot of Ralph. Besides, suppose they get tired of him after a week? Then what?

▲ We won't, we promise! Oh, come on, Dad! Wouldn't it be nice to be greeted by Ralph, wagging his tail? Just think of the love and affection . . .

○ I have a family for love and affection.

● It *would* help Ted out. . . .

○ I can see I'm outnumbered. O.K., I give in, as long as no one makes *me* do anything.

Figure it out

1. Find at least three arguments in the conversation for keeping Ralph and three against keeping him.

2. Fill in the blanks with *the* or nothing.

1. I don't want Ralph. _____ dog has a miserable personality.
2. Our landlord is afraid of _____ dogs.
3. You should give your children _____ responsibility.
4. Just think of _____ affection that Ralph would show us.
5. I get _____ affection from my family.
6. I think _____ pets are a lot of work.

Ways to say it

PERSUADE SOMEONE

A. Find these expressions in the conversation on p. 20, and notice how they are used. (All of them except *What if...?* appear.)

Make another point	Suggest a possibility
Besides ... What's more ... In any case ...	Suppose (that) ... ? What if ... ?
State a reservation	State a condition
True, but ...	As long as ...

> Use a past form with *Suppose ... ?* and *What if ... ?* when the possibility is contrary-to-fact. Compare:
>
> Suppose Victor *is* at home? (He might be.)
> Suppose Victor *were* rich? (He's not.)

B. You and your partner are going to spend a week with some friends who live in another city. The trip takes ten hours by car. One of you would like to drive the ten hours in one day. The other would rather break the trip into two days. Persuade your partner of your view, using the arguments in the box. Use the expressions in Part A to connect your ideas.

Some arguments
We'd get there sooner. We'd have more time with our friends. We wouldn't waste two whole days getting there. We wouldn't have to spend money on a hotel.	◄ one day
Getting there could be part of the fun. We could take our time and enjoy the trip. We could stay in an inexpensive place. We'd get there more rested.	◄ two days

> You may say:
>
> We'*d* get there sooner (if we *drove* there in one day).
> We'*ll* get there sooner (if we *drive* there in one day).

 PERSUADE SOMEONE

Complete the sentences. Another student will try to persuade you to change your mind about two of them.

- One thing I'll never buy is a car. As long as I live near town, I don't need one. Besides, I hate to drive. It makes me nervous.
- Yes, but maybe it makes you nervous because you're not used to it. Suppose you drove more? You might start to enjoy it.
- Hmm ... that's a good point. I hadn't thought of that....

Some expressions
That's a good point.   Maybe you're right.   I'm still not convinced.

1. One thing I'll never buy is _____ .
2. I can't understand why people spend their money on _____ .
3. One place I have no desire to visit is _____ .
4. _____ is something I have no interest in.

Your partner has trouble speaking in public. You once took the "Speak Effectively" course. Try to persuade your partner to take the course, too, using these expressions:

1. It helped me _____ .
2. They had us _____ .
3. They let us _____ .
4. It made me _____ .

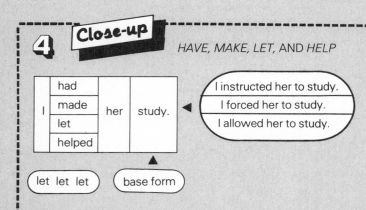

Speak Effectively!

Do you get "butterflies" in your stomach whenever you have to speak in front of a group? Do you hate making speeches? Are you shy?

Our course will help you get over your nervousness and develop self-confidence. We'll have you write speeches and then, in a safe, supportive environment, we'll let you try them out on your classmates. Most important, we'll make you realize that you *can* be an effective speaker.

Sign up today. Write or call:

**The Spring School of Speech
85 Chelsea St.
Los Angeles, California 90052
(213) 555-9835**

---

4 **Close-up**   *HAVE, MAKE, LET,* AND *HELP*

	had		
I	made	her	study.
	let		
	helped		

(let let let)   (base form)

▶ I instructed her to study.
I forced her to study.
I allowed her to study.

Make can also be used to mean *cause*:
The course *made* me feel confident. = It *caused* me to feel confident.

Make is often used with adjectives to mean *cause*:
John *made* me angry. = He *caused* me to be angry.

---

 5 PERSUADE SOMEONE

Rewrite the advertisement, completing it by filling in the blanks with *have, make, let,* or *help*. Some items have two answers.

Get into shape at the Body Factory!

It's work, yes. Our instructors are tough, and they'll work harder than ever. But you'll have a good time, too. The time will fly and the work will seem like fun. Our instructors will _____ you do exercises that you'll actually enjoy.

One of our experts will work with you to design a diet just for your needs. We won't _____ you give up everything you like to eat, either. Most important, we'll _____ you stick to your diet and lose those unwanted pounds.

As a special introductory offer, we'll _____ you come in and try our program for one week at *no cost!*

For more information, write or call: The Body Factory, 24 Main St., St. Paul, Minnesota 55101, (314) 555-9820

 **Close-up**   *THE*

He's afraid of	dogs. the dogs next door.	◄ count noun
I hate	coffee. the coffee at Ray's Coffee Shop.	◄ mass noun
Dogs need	love. the love of their owners.	◄ abstract noun
I studied	Chinese.	◄ language
I get along well with	Mexicans. the Chinese.	◄ people
I used to live in I have cousins in	Greece. the United States.	◄ country

When a count noun is the subject of a sentence, either a singular or plural noun may be used to make a generalization:

A dog is a lot of trouble.
Dogs are a lot of trouble.

Use *the* before the people of a country only when the word is not made plural by adding an *s*.
the Chinese   *the* French

Use *the* only before countries whose name is plural or contains *United*, *Union*, or *Republic*:
the Netherlands   *the* Dominican Republic

---

7 GIVE AN OPINION

Fill in the blanks with *a(n), the*, or nothing, and then complete the sentences. You may want to use some of the nouns in the box. Share your opinions with another student, who will either agree or disagree with them.

1. When I was _____ child, my parents never let me ...   I (don't) think _____ parents should let _____ children ...
2. My father always made me ...   I (don't) think _____ parent should make _____ child ...
3. In my opinion, _____ children need ...
4. ...is something _____ child often does not get enough of.
5. ...are _____ qualities I value most in _____ people.

Some abstract nouns			
love	freedom	generosity	courage
affection	discipline	ambition	tenderness
guidance	approval	intelligence	independence
responsibility	loyalty	honesty	patience

8 SUPPORT AN OPINION

Write a paragraph supporting one of the opinions you gave in exercise 7. Include at least three arguments in favor of your opinion.

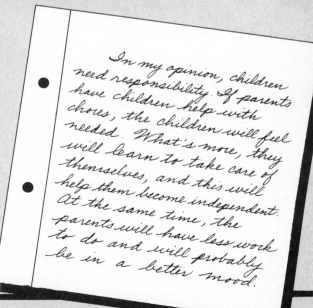

In my opinion, children need responsibility. If parents have children help with chores, the children will feel needed. What's more, they will learn to take care of themselves, and this will help them become independent. At the same time, the parents will have less work to do and will probably be in a better mood.

23

Your turn

1.

There is a large vacant lot near your house, and the city is trying to decide how to use the land. You are at a community meeting, which was planned so you and others in the neighborhood could present your views. Look at the photos, which show the different possibilities under consideration for the land. What do you think your neighborhood needs most? Why? Work in groups and try to persuade the other people at the meeting of your opinion.

the vacant lot

an art museum

a community center

2. Listen in 📼

Read the questions below. Then listen to the radio editorial and answer the questions.

1. What other words or expressions does Mr. Spector use to refer to teenagers?
2. What does Mr. Spector think the city should do with the lot?
3. What is one argument Mr. Spector gives to support his opinion?

3.

Has the editorial you heard changed your opinion about the vacant lot in your neighborhood? Discuss this question in groups.

4. On your own

Write one of the letters described below.

1. Write an answer to William Spector's editorial. Try to persuade him that the city should do something else with the lot.
2. Write a letter to the appropriate official in your town, giving your opinion on the lot. Try to be persuasive by including as many arguments as you can to support your opinion.

a castle

an apartment building

a parking lot

a public garden

an office building

RKO 86TH ST. TWIN

a movie theater

a hospital

25

Meet the Oldest Man

by

Dick Schaap

He was 9 years old the year Gandhi was born, 14 the year Churchill was born, 29 the year Hitler was born. He married for the first time when he was 50. He married for the third time when he was 92. When he was 100, he took five-mile walks, and he rode a bicycle until he was 110. He worked until he was 116. At 122, he took his first flight in a jet. And at 123, admitting that his eyesight wasn't what it used to be, he had an operation for cataracts.

Arthur Reed was born June 28, 1860, in Buffalo, New York, and lives now, at 123, in Oakland, California. He is a widower for the third time. He is retired, finally, and his health, logically, is not the best. His eyesight remains poor, and so does his hearing. He suffers from arthritis. He has no teeth, which makes some of his words hard to understand, but his voice is still strong and resonant. And his brown eyes dance under white eyebrows when he says, "All I want is to get ...a little money, and a new wife, and go to New York."

To meet Arthur Reed is to encounter history: a black man born in the days of slavery, a man born before Edison's first light bulb, who now enjoys watching baseball games and boxing matches on television. "I hate the rest of the junk on TV," he says.

Arthur Reed celebrating his 123rd birthday with Weldon Russell.

Arthur Reed is 123 years old and feels good. He's never smoked. He had his last drink in 1898. He doesn't want anything in him, he says, that makes it so that he can't pick up what he drops.

There is some question as to Arthur's real age, however. His birth records were destroyed in a fire, and *The Guinness Book of World Records* says that a Japanese man named Shigechiyo Izumi, 118 years old, is the world's oldest man. But it's probably safe to say that Reed is the oldest man alive in the United States. He has lived under 25 of the United States' 40 Presidents. He has lived in or visited 44 of the 50 states, some of them before they became states. He never had children, and over the years he lost track of his brother and two sisters.

He worked as a cotton picker, carpenter, bricklayer, and truck driver. In 1928, he went to California and got a job at the Phoenix Iron Works. Even during his 70s and 80s, he was much like other men at the plant who had been working there for decades. His friend Weldon Russell remembers that there were many 80-year-olds working there. "They were men, like Arthur, who had worked hard all their lives. They never got sick. They were always in good shape."

In his 90s, Reed would bicycle from Oakland to Fresno, a good 100 miles, and work the cotton fields. When he was 95, he told Weldon Russell that he'd really like two things: a new suit and a hole in the ground. Weldon got him the new suit but decided to wait on the hole in the ground. No sense hurrying things.

How do you get to be 123? Arthur Reed laughs and gives the answer he has been giving every year since people began celebrating his birthday with questions about longevity. "They made me out of good dirt," he says.

Editor's Note: This article was written in 1983. Arthur Reed died in the summer of 1984 at the reported age of 124.

Figure it out

1. **The man described in this article is a black man from the United States who was 123 years old when he was interviewed. As you read the article, try to figure out the answers to these questions. When you have finished, adjust your answers if necessary.**

1. What are some ways that life has changed since Arthur Reed was born? What clue does the article give that life for blacks in the United States was very different 123 years ago?
2. Does the article give advice on how to live a long life or does it only present one man's story? If you feel the article makes generalizations, say what they are.
3. Aside from his age, what are some ways that Arthur Reed was unusual?

2. **Find another way to say it.**

1. He has stopped working.
2. His third wife has died.
3. His voice is still strong and clear.
4. He went somewhere by plane for the first time.
5. He still can't see very well.
6. Their health was always good.
7. There's no reason to hurry.
8. He stopped keeping in touch with his brother and two sisters.

3. **The suffix *-er* changes verbs into nouns that mean "a person who." It is often used to form noun compounds: A *truck driver* is someone who drives a truck. Using the information in the article, complete the paragraph with nouns ending in *-er*.**

Arthur Reed's good health and longevity were very unusual. In his 90s, he would bicycle from Oakland to Fresno to work as a _____ . Reed had once been a _____ , and he was used to being on the road. He was also good with his hands and had worked as both a _____ and a _____ .

I remember . . .

Try this

Tell another student about an older person you know or knew, such as one of your grandparents or great-grandparents.

Bess Anderson is visiting her father, Charles Anderson, in Michigan. Bess's father is a widower.

● Bess Anderson
○ Charles Anderson

● Dad, have you ever given any thought to moving south, to one of those retirement communities? It would be warm, you'd be with other people . . .

○ I'm not interested in picking up and moving away.

● But don't you get tired of fighting the cold?

○ Oh, I'm used to it. In fact, I've always liked the winter. I remember those cold winter nights when you and Jim were kids. We used to sit around the fireplace, the four of us. Outside the snow would be falling and the wind would be howling, but it was warm and cozy inside. I can still see your mother sitting in her rocking chair knitting.

● I always hated to get out of bed in the winter. The floor was so cold.

○ And when you finally *did* get up, you were always so late you never had time to finish your breakfast.

● Well, I wasn't really that crazy about oatmeal.

○ Off you and Jim would go, bundled up like two little Eskimos. Your mother would stand at the door and tell you to hurry or you'd miss the bus.

● We did once, you know. We were so afraid to tell you we decided to walk the five miles to school through the snow. Luckily, Mr. Fleming came along in his truck and gave us a ride.

○ (*Speaking softly*) Yes, there are a lot of memories in this house.

Figure it out

Find these sentences in the conversation. Then say *present, future, one time in the past,* or *often in the past.*

1. We used to sit around the fireplace.
2. I'm used to it.
3. You'd be with other people.
4. Your mother would stand at the door.
5. Mr. Fleming came along in his truck.
6. You never had time to finish your breakfast.

Ways to say it

1 RECALL THE PAST

Describe a former time in your life to another student.

When my brother and I were growing up, we used to spend summers with my grandparents in Tunisia. Every morning, we'd walk through the market place on our way to the beach, and I remember so well the smells of spices and the bright colors of the fabrics. Then my brother and I would swim, and my grandfather would stand near the water with his pants legs rolled up and watch us. He wanted to make sure we didn't swim out too far. I can still hear him calling to us when we were only three meters from the edge, "O.K., that's enough! Come back now!"

Use *used to* or *would* to talk about repeated activities in the past. If it is clear that the activity was repeated, you may also use the simple past.

Notice how the present participle is used with sense verbs:

I can still *see* my grandfather *standing* near the water.
I can *hear* him *calling* to us.

Some topics

a typical day or weekend when you were a child
special occasions during your childhood, such as summers or holidays
your student days
your early married life

Some ways to begin

When I was growing up . . .
During my childhood . . .
Every summer . . .
When I first got married . . .

A *souk*, or market, in Tunisia.

2 RECALL THE PAST

Describe a specific experience in your past to another student.

A few years ago, I went back to Tunisia. It was September, so most of the tourists had already gone home. I visited the familiar places—the beaches, houses, cafés—the places where I had spent so many happy hours with family and friends. It was a quiet moment, a sweet one.

You can use the simple past, past continuous, or past perfect to set the scene for your story:
It *was* September.
It *was raining*.
The tourists *had gone*.

Use the simple past to tell what happened:
I *went back* to Tunisia.

Some ways to begin

A few years ago, I . . .
I remember one time I . . .
Once I . . .
Not long ago I . . .
One day I . . .

3

THE PAST HABITUAL

Used to	Would	Simple past
Use *used to* to talk about repeated activities: 　I *used to* go to the beach every day.	Use *would* to talk about repeated activities when you are continuing a discussion in the past: 　I *used to* spend a lot of time outdoors. I'*d* go to the beach every day. Because of its conditional meaning, do not use *would* to start a discussion of the past: 　I'*d* go to the beach every day (if I had time).	Use the simple past to talk about a specific experience: 　Yesterday, I *went* to the beach (once). When a frequency expression shows that an activity was repeated, you may use the simple past: 　When I was a child, I *went* to the beach *every day*. Use the simple past after *when, before,* and *after*: 　*When* I *came* home from school, I'd do my chores.
Use *used to* with verbs such as *have, live, want,* and *like,* which express continuity but do not refer to repeated activities: 　I *used to live* in Rio. 　I *used to like* to swim.	Use *would* only with verbs that refer to repeated activities. When used with other verbs, *would* has a conditional meaning: 　I'*d live* in Rio (if I could).	Use the simple past when it is clear that you are expressing continuity: 　I *lived* in Rio *for six years.* 　I *never liked* to swim.

4 DESCRIBE THE PAST

Rewrite the beginning of this chapter, completing it by using the verbs in parentheses appropriately. In some cases, you may use *would, used to,* or the simple past. In other cases, only one or two of these are appropriate.

feed　fed　fed

Chapter One

_____

　　When my grandfather _____ a boy, he _____ on a farm. (be, live)　He _____ at four in the morning to do his chores. (get up)　First he _____ the cows and then he _____ the chickens. (milk, feed)　Sometimes he _____ the wood. (chop)　After he _____ his chores, he _____ seven miles to school. (finish, walk)

　　My grandfather never _____ to get up early. (like)　From the time he was fourteen, he only _____ of one thing — the city. (think)　As soon as he _____ his eighteenth birthday, he _____ the farm and _____ a job in a factory. (reach, leave, get)　That's where he _____ my grandmother. (meet)　The two of them _____ home together every day after work. (walk)

5 RECALL THE PAST

Look at exercises 1 and 2 again and reread the stories told by the person from Tunisia. Then write your own story recalling a time in your life and a specific experience from that time. In the first paragraph, give a general description (as you did in exercise 1). In the second, describe a specific event (as you did in exercise 2).

6 SOME VERBS AND EXPRESSIONS FOLLOWED BY PREPOSITIONS

I dream I think I worry I often talk I'm nervous I'm excited	about	moving to Europe. going to Italy. saving money. leaving home. taking a trip. going away.
I'm interested I believe	in	teaching Spanish. helping people.

I'm afraid I'm tired I'm proud I'm jealous	of	living alone. being a student. having a good job. people who travel.
I'm satisfied	with	earning a small salary.

All of these expressions can be followed by nouns, as well as gerunds:

I often *dream about* my grandfather.
I'm *proud of* my children.

The word *get* may be used with many of the expressions above to mean *become*:

I *got tired of* waiting, so I went home.
I'*m getting nervous about* our exam tomorrow.

7 TALK ABOUT HOW YOU'VE CHANGED

Use the expressions in exercise 6 and any others you know to talk about how you've changed over the years.

● I used to be very interested in philosophy. It fascinated me, and I never got tired of talking about the meaning of life. Now I don't have time to worry about such things. I'm more interested in practical problems.

○ I've become more practical, too. I never used to think about my career. I would take odd jobs when I needed money. I believed in having a good time, and I never worked very hard. Now I think about the future a lot more....

Your turn

1.

Interview someone in your community who is elderly and find out what life was like when he or she was young. You may choose to interview a relative, a neighbor, a friend, or anyone else you know. Make sure to take notes so you don't forget the details. Then share the story with a group of classmates. Here are some questions to ask during your interview:

1. Do these pictures bring back any memories? What household appliances were common in your home when you were young?
2. How were young people different? What did they talk and think about most?
3. What was a typical day like when you were a child?
4. What are your most vivid memories of your childhood? Could you tell me about some of your experiences?

5. What did your parents do? How were working conditions different from the way they are today?
6. How is life easier today? Can you think of some ways that it's harder?
7. If you had to choose one way that life has changed most over the years, what would it be?

2. Listen in 📼

Edna Olden, a sixty-five-year-old woman, is describing her mother's life as a young woman. Read the questions below about Edna Olden's mother. Then listen to the conversation and answer the questions.

1. What did she want most when she was young?
2. What kind of work did she do?
3. What did she have to do when she came home?
4. What was the Oldens' apartment like?

3. On your own

Write a short article, choosing one of the topics below.

1. Your local newspaper has asked you to write about the person you interviewed. Describe his or her past, using the information from your interview.
2. You think life was easier (or harder) when you were a child. Support your argument by describing your childhood.

an oil-burning lamp

a high-wheeler bicycle

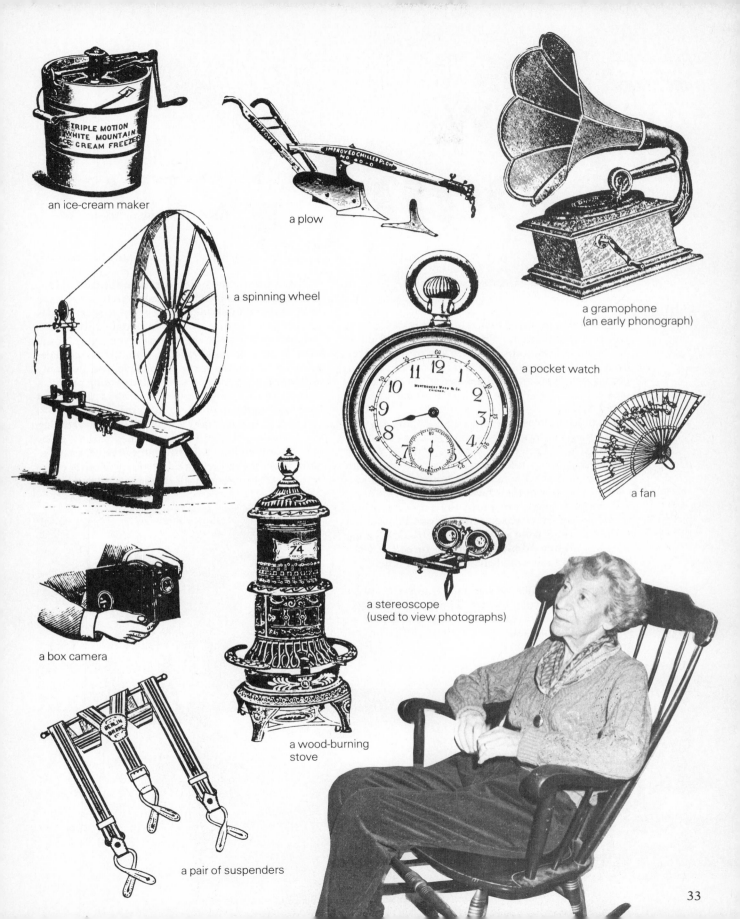

an ice-cream maker

a plow

a gramophone
(an early phonograph)

a spinning wheel

a pocket watch

a fan

a box camera

a wood-burning
stove

a stereoscope
(used to view photographs)

a pair of suspenders

33

THE NEW
Soap Gener

by Manuela Soares

It has been reported that at noon each day, a large number of students at Princeton University come out of their classrooms and go to any convenient television set available. With great works of science, philosophy, history, and literature still in their arms, they watch *The Young and the Restless* in fascinated silence.

In colleges across the United States, the daytime serial drama known as the soap opera has suddenly become "in." Between the hours of 11 A.M. and 4:30 P.M., college television lounges are filled with soap opera fans who can't wait to see the next episode in the lives of their favorite characters.

Actually, soaps are more than a college fad; they're a youth fad. When school is out, high-school students are in front of their TV sets. One young working woman admitted that she turned down a higher paying job rather than give up watching her favorite serials.

During the 1960's, it was uncommon for young people to watch soap operas. The mood of the sixties was very different from now. It was a time of seriousness, and talk was about social issues of great importance.

Now, seriousness has been replaced by fun. Young people want to be happy. It may seem strange that they should turn to soap opera, which is known for showing trouble in people's lives. But soap opera is enjoyment. Young people can identify with the soap opera character, who, like the college-age viewer, is looking for happy love, and probably not finding it. And soap opera gives young people a chance to feel close to people without having to bear any responsibility for their problems.

The fact that so many young people are watching the soaps has changed soap opera. The most obvious difference now is in the age of the characters. "It seems they're getting rid of all my favorite characters and bringing in all these new young kids,"

ation

complained one long-time viewer. Now all shows have at least a few characters between the ages of fifteen and twenty-five who are central figures in the drama. Young people can identify with the situations young characters find themselves in—conflicts with parents, career-identity crises, first loves.

Producers and writers are trying to make soaps more "meaningful" to young people in another way: by dealing with social issues they think are of importance to them. These issues are usually presented on the level that all other soap opera matters are presented: the emotional level. In the past, soap characters have tended to feel rather than figure out, and for the most part, that is still true.

There is a value system in soap opera characterizations, one that is very attractive to young people. One of the principal values is honesty. There also seems to be a suspicion of wealth.

But perhaps the main appeal is that soap operas show the difficulties of life and love. There are no easy answers in daytime drama. One of the "messages" of soap opera is that getting hurt is a part of life.

Figure It Out

1. **Before starting to read, look at the photos and the title of the article. What do you think the article is about? Does your opinion change after you have read the first paragraph?**

2. **As you read, try to figure out the answers to these questions. When you have finished, adjust your answers if necessary.**

1. What is a soap opera? How would you explain what one is to someone who didn't know?
2. Why do young people like soap operas?
3. How have soap opera producers and writers tried to appeal to young people?
4. What is one important theme of many soap operas?

3. **Skim the article again and say *Right* or *Wrong* for each statement below. Correct the wrong statements.**

1. *The Young and the Restless* is a novel.
2. Fewer young people are watching soap operas than ever before.
3. Soap operas emphasize that people should be honest and that money is not all that important.
4. Most soap opera characters are happy and in love.
5. Soap operas never deal with the society the characters live in.

4. **Most adjectives ending in -nt can be changed into nouns by dropping the -t and adding -ce, as in the adjective *important* and the noun *importance*. Fill in each blank with an appropriate adjective or noun. All of the words you will need were used in the article.**

More young people are watching soap operas than ever before and, as a result, the soap operas themselves are very _____ from those of twenty years ago. The most obvious _____ is that the characters are younger. But, in addition, writers have started to appeal to young people by dealing with social issues of _____ to them. Young people, in turn, have reacted enthusiastically. College students make sure their classes are at _____ times, so they won't miss their favorite programs. During the day, television lounges are crowded with fans who sit in _____ as they follow the lives of the characters they have come to know so well.

The problem is . . .

Everyone has problems. You might have problems at school or work, or with your parents or children. Choose a partner and discuss some problems that you or someone you know has.

Watching TV can take your mind off your problems.

A
- ● I've been worried about Ricky, Mrs. Rosen.
- ○ What seems to be the problem?
- ● Well, he has trouble concentrating . . . his mind wanders. And he's not getting along with the other children. I was wondering if there might be something on his mind, some problem at home. . . . (*Changes channel*)

B
- ▲ I can't take it anymore. That man drove me crazy yesterday. First he wants one thing, then he wants something completely different. And to make matters worse, he makes up his mind at ten to five. I wish he'd make his decisions earlier in the day. Now who walked off with my stapler? It makes me so mad when . . .
- △ Oh, I've got it. Here. (*Changes channel*)

C
- ■ Do you ever have days when you just can't cope?
- □ Oh, sure. What you need on days like that is for someone to pat you on the back and say, "Cheer up!"
- ■ I wish it were that simple. Bill's folks are visiting us, and they're really starting to get on my nerves. His mother's always going around cleaning. . . .
- □ And you're complaining? I'd love it.
- ■ Not if you'd just cleaned the same room. They're always criticizing me and giving me advice. And let me tell you, there's not much we see eye to eye on.
- □ Well, what can I say? Cheer up!

Figure it out

1. Which conversation involves a problem at work? Say *A*, *B*, or *C*.

2. Which sentence in each pair shows a negative attitude on the part of the speaker? Choose *a* or *b*.

1. a. They're always giving me advice.
   b. They always give me advice.

2. a. First he told me to file. Then he wanted me to type.
   b. First he tells me to file. Then he suddenly wants me to type.

Ways to say it

1 SCOLD SOMEONE

Play the role of each of these people and say something objectionable. Your partner will guess which person you have chosen and scold you with the response under the picture.

You're always complaining.

You're always criticizing me.

You're always changing your mind. First you say you want coffee, then tea, and now . . .

You're always making fun of people.

2 TALK ABOUT RELATIONSHIPS WITH PEOPLE

Talk about your relationship with a member of your family, a friend, a coworker, or anyone else you know.

- How do you get along with your boss?
○ We get along well. He's easy to work with.
- You're lucky. My boss is always looking over my shoulder to see what I'm doing. It really gets on my nerves.
○ I can see why. It would drive me crazy.

Some ways of relating
We get along well (with each other).
We work well together.
He's easy (hard) to work with.
We agree on everything.
We don't see eye to eye on anything.
We can't stand each other.

Some reactions
He drives me crazy. (informal)
She gets on my nerves. (informal)
It makes me mad (when) . . . (informal)
It hurts my feelings (when) . . .

3 PRESENT CONTINUOUS AND SIMPLE PRESENT: SPECIAL USES

Present continuous

He always gives me advice. I really appreciate it.
He's *always giving* me advice. It gets on my nerves.

▲

In general, use the simple present with frequency adverbs. However, if your attitude is negative, you may use the present continuous with *always*.

Simple present

First she asked me to type the letters. Then she had me take them to the post office.
First she *asks* me to type the letters. Then she suddenly *changes* her mind and *has* me file.

▲

In general, use the past tense to show a sequence of events in the past. However, sometimes you may use the present, especially to tell about an irritating or humorous incident.

4 Put the verbs in parentheses into the simple present, the present continuous, or the past tense. Use the frequency adverbs when they are given. Make sure to consider the attitude of the speaker. When the attitude is negative, there are two possible answers.

1. My parents are pretty understanding. They _____ to me and _____ to see things from my point of view. (always listen, try)

2. I can't figure my parents out. First they _____ me to look for a job over the summer. (tell) Then when I _____ one, they _____ that they _____ me to work at their store. (find, decide, want) They _____ their minds. (always change)

3. My English teacher is so nice. First she _____ us homework for the weekend. (give) Then she _____ to give us the weekend off. (decide)

4. My son is a complete mystery to me. He _____ that he has nothing to do. (always complain) Then, yesterday his friend _____ him to go to the movies and he _____ he _____ too tired. (call, say, be)

5 MAKE WISHES

Complete the following sentences and give a reason for each wish. Your partner will respond appropriately.

● I wish I were younger. I'd have more energy, and I wouldn't get tired so easily.
○ I know what you mean....

1. I wish I were _____ .
2. I wish I weren't _____ .
3. I wish I had _____ .
4. I wish I didn't have to _____ .
5. I wish I could _____ .
6. I wish my parents (wife, husband, children) would _____ .

6 Close-up   *WISH:* PRESENT AND FUTURE TIME

Present or future tense

| Life is hard. |
| I don't have much time. |
| I can't speak French. |

| I can't go to the movie tonight. |
| I'm not going to be there later. |
| She won't decide until Friday. |

Past tense form referring to present or future

I wish	life weren't so hard.
	I had more time.
	I could speak French.

◀ wishes about the present

I wish	I could go to the movie tonight.
	I were going to be there later.
	she would (she'd) decide tomorrow.

◀ wishes about the future

For actions that take place in the present but may be repeated in the future, you may express your wish in two ways:

He yells at me a lot. I wish he *didn't* yell at me so much.
He yells at me a lot. I wish he *wouldn't* yell at me so much.

7 TALK ABOUT PROBLEMS

Change the numbered sentences so that they are wishes. Some items have two answers.

We're worried about Susie.
1. She isn't doing well in school.
   We wish she were ...
2. She doesn't get along with her classmates.
3. She doesn't talk to us about her problems.
4. She keeps everything inside.

I've got a real problem with my neighbors.
5. They play their stereo at all hours of the day and night.
6. They keep all their windows open, too.
7. They aren't very considerate.

8 TALK ABOUT A PROBLEM

Tell your partner about an imaginary or real problem at home, at school, or at work. Your partner will show sympathy, cheer you up, or give you advice.

- I just can't seem to have a conversation with my father. The problem is he's always interrupting me. He never lets me finish a sentence.
○ That can be frustrating.
- It sure is! And to make matters worse, he never listens to my point of view.
○ Hmm ... I'd suggest ...

Some expressions
I (just) can't seem to ...
He's always ...
I have trouble ...
It makes it difficult to ... when ...
First he ..., then he ...
I wish ...

Some ways to connect your ideas
The problem is ...
The worst part is ...
To make matters worse ...

Your turn

1.

You and a group of your classmates work for a market research company, and you are studying which brands of cookies and crackers are selling well. Each of you has a different task, such as writing letters or making telephone calls. One member of your group, David Foster, is supposed to write letters to stores, but he's been causing problems. Look at the pictures and discuss what some of these problems are. Then try to decide what to do. Here are some of your options:

1. Write a memo to David.
2. Have one person talk to David.
3. Talk to David as a group.
4. Complain about David to your supervisor.

2. On your own

Write an entry in your diary, choosing one of these options:

1. It's been a hard and frustrating week for you because of your problems at work with David Foster. Tell your diary about them.
2. Tell your diary about a real problem you're having. Maybe you'll feel better.

3. Listen in 📼

Read the statement below. Then listen to the conversation and choose *a*, *b*, or *c*.

David Foster has had trouble working because _____ .

a. he isn't interested in market research anymore
b. he's been worried about his health
c. he's been worried about losing his job

4.

Has your opinion of David Foster changed? Why or why not? Discuss this question in groups.

Man Climbs 110-Story Tower

by Mary Breasted

NEW YORK, May 26 — Using equipment he built himself and tested in secret at night, a 27-year-old toymaker and mountain climber from Queens climbed the South Tower of the World Trade Center yesterday morning to the delight of the thousands of people who watched his three-and-a-half-hour effort.

As he safely reached the top of the tower at 10:05 A.M., the climber turned to wave to the cheering crowd 110 stories — 411.48 meters (1,350 feet) — below.

The climber, George H. Willig, was arrested by the police and sued for $250,000 by New York City for his illegal adventure.

But to the people on the street he was a hero.

"It was a personal challenge," Mr. Willig said when people asked him why he had done it. "I just wanted the prize of get-ting to the top." The climb started at 6:30 A.M. At first, the police and the spectators thought that perhaps Mr. Willig was insane. An expert suicide rescuer tried to persuade him to climb onto a window-washing scaffold lowered from the roof.

He continued, however, and as the minutes passed and he became tinier and tinier inching up the silver wall, Mr. Willig won the hearts of all below and was cheered and applauded on his way.

And when it was announced to reporters soon after the climb that the city was suing Mr. Willig for all the expense and trouble he had caused, the reporters booed loudly.

Eighty police officers had to be taken away from their other jobs to control the crowds and traffic in the downtown area during Mr. Willig's climb. In addition, a police helicopter had to chase away six other helicopters circling the World Trade Center towers and sometimes getting dangerously close, probably hired by news organizations.

The two police officers who arrested Mr. Willig, congratulated him when he had finished his climb. Officer Dewitt C. Allen was full of admiration for Mr. Willig, who, he said, "was in fantastic shape."

He reached Mr. Willig's level — then the fifty-fifth floor — at about 8:30, riding on the window-washing scaffold. With him was Officer Glenn Kilidare, who, Officer Allen said, "was a little afraid of heights."

After about three minutes of conversation, Officer Allen realized that Mr. Willig was not insane.

"I judged by his responses to my questions, by the type of equipment he was using, and I guess you could say by the look in his eyes," Officer Allen continued.

"Every response he gave me was reasonable. The only thing unreasonable about it was the fact that he was on the outside of the building."

"I've been in situations a lot scarier," said the small, bearded Mr. Willig, an experienced mountain climber.

Mr. Willig had planned the World Trade Center expedition for a year and had tested the devices he used "four or five times at night," but never actually had climbed "until today."

The police allowed the media to look at Mr. Willig's equipment, but would not let them take photographs of it for fear that someone might try to copy it.

Figure it out

1. Before you read the article, think of possible answers to these questions. Then, as you read, look for the correct answers. When you have finished reading, answer the questions.

1. Why did George Willig climb the 110-story tower in the photo?
2. What was the reaction of the police and of people in the street?

2. Choose *a*, *b*, or *c*, or a combination of these. Find the sentences in the article that support your answers.

1. Officer Allen knew Willig wasn't crazy by
   _____ .
   a. the way Willig answered his questions
   b. the look in Willig's eyes
   c. the way Willig wore his hair

2. The police tried to persuade Willig to stop his climb because _____ .
   a. he was wasting many officers' time and the city's money
   b. reporters were angry and were booing loudly
   c. his equipment was dangerous

3. After the event, police officers _____ .
   a. made Willig pay them for their trouble
   b. told reporters to photograph Willig's equipment
   c. arrested Willig

4. Willig climbed the tower because _____ .
   a. he wanted a new challenge
   b. he hoped to make a lot of money
   c. he had climbed the tower before and enjoyed doing it

3. The prefixes *in-* and *un-* both make adjectives negative. The prefix *in-* becomes *im-* when followed by the letters *p* or *b*, *il-* when followed by the letter *l*, and *ir-* when followed by the letter *r*. Write sentences about George Willig using each of these words.:

insane   illegal   irresponsible   unafraid   unreasonable   unsafe

Did I ever tell you . . . ?

Try this

Have you ever had an exciting adventure or a very frightening experience? Tell another student about it.

Anne Christopher is telling two of her friends about a frightening experience she once had.

- Anne Christopher
- Maria Diaz
- ▲ Steven Wong

● Did I ever tell you about the time I almost drowned in a cave?

○ No! How horrible! What were you doing in a cave?

● Tom Riley and I used to go cave exploring a lot.

▲ Oh, wait . . . I think I've heard this story. Didn't you go into a cave when it was raining?

● Well, it wasn't raining when we went in. In fact, they'd predicted good weather the day before. The rain just came out of nowhere once we'd been in the cave for an hour or so. And water started rushing in.

○ You must have been terrified.

● Well, I wasn't exactly thrilled. Especially when I looked down and saw the water level rising fast.

○ What did you do?

● Tom and I separated and climbed up onto the highest places we could find. Of course, it was dark except for our flashlights. All of a sudden, I heard Tom scream.

▲ Oh, yeah, a bat swooped down in his face, right?

○ I would have died.

● Believe me, it was a close call. Fortunately, it didn't rain long, but we still had to wait there for hours for the water level to go down. And the bat was flying around the whole time.

○ What a frightening experience that must have been!

● Well, looking back on it, it seems exciting. But I must admit I was pretty scared at the time.

Figure it out

1. Choose *a* or *b* for each sentence.

a. The sentence describes an event.
b. The sentence describes a continuous action or situation.

1. Tom screamed.
2. The water was rising.
3. A bat swooped down.
4. It wasn't raining.

2. Join each pair of sentences with *before* or *after*.

1. We decided to go cave exploring. They'd predicted good weather.
2. It started to rain. We'd been in the cave for about an hour.
3. We'd already been in the cave for hours. The water level started to go down.

Ways to say it

1 REACT TO AN EVENT

Put the verbs in parentheses into the simple past or the past continuous. Your partner will react appropriately.

- Did I ever tell you about the time I went cave exploring and almost drowned?
- No! How horrible! How did it happen? . . .

1. I _____ cave exploring and almost _____ . (go, drown)
2. I _____ in a department store, and Michael Jackson _____ to buy some gloves. (shop, come in)
3. A tree _____ on my car during a snowstorm and completely _____ it. (fall, destroy)
4. I _____ to give a speech in front of two hundred people and _____ I _____ two different socks.
   (get up, notice, wear)
5. I _____ dinner when a tarantula _____ across my plate. (eat, walk)
6. I _____ a race because I _____ just before the finish line. (lose, fall down)

fall	fell	fallen
wear	wore	worn

Some reactions	
How	horrible!
What a	frightening experience!
That must have been	terrifying!
You must have been	terrified!
I would have been	very upset!
I would have	died (panicked, fainted)!

Some present and past participles	
depressing	depressed
disappointing	disappointed
embarrassing	embarrassed
exciting	excited
frustrating	frustrated
terrifying	terrified

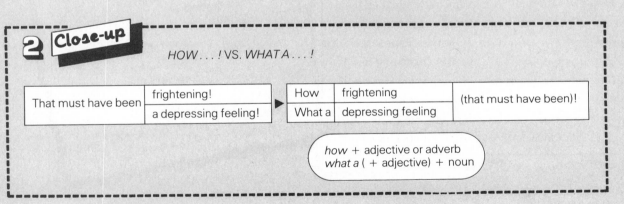

2 **Close-up**

HOW . . . ! VS. WHAT A . . . !

That must have been	frightening!
	a depressing feeling!

▶

How	frightening	(that must have been)!
What a	depressing feeling	

how + adjective or adverb
what a (+ adjective) + noun

**3** REACT TO A STORY

Tell another student about a personal experience you've had. You may choose one that was exciting, dangerous, funny, embarrassing, or disappointing. Your partner will react, using adjectives and nouns from the box or any others that are appropriate.

- I hadn't seen my old friend Pablo in twenty years. He was my boyfriend in high school, but we never kept in touch. Then one day I ran into him in a movie theater.
- What a strange experience that must have been!
- It sure was! We found we have even more in common now. We're going out again.
- How incredible! . . .

Some adjectives	Some nouns
embarrassing	situation
disappointing	story
funny	ending
strange	experience
incredible	problem
terrible	reaction
depressing	feeling

4 **Close-up**

SIMPLE PAST VS. PAST PERFECT VS. PAST CONTINUOUS

Use the simple past to report an event in the past: 　A toymaker *climbed* the World Trade Center yesterday.
Use the past perfect to report a situation or an event that ended before another point in the past: 　He*'d* never *climbed* it before.
Use the past continuous to describe the situation at the time of an event in the past: 　He *was climbing* the tower when the police arrived.

5 TELL A STORY

Rewrite the articles, putting the verbs in parentheses into the simple past, the past perfect, or the past continuous.

Man Climbs 110-Story Tower

NEW YORK, May 26—A 27-year-old toymaker from Queens _____ the South Tower of the World Trade Center yesterday morning. (climb)　Thousands of delighted spectators _____ the three-and-a-half-half-hour event. (watch)　The climber, George H. Willig, _____ the expedition for a year and _____ his devices four or five times but never actually _____ the tower until yesterday. (plan, test, climb)

Skater Has Close Call

AMSTERDAM, Netherlands—Champion skater Mary Van Dine _____ on a pond near her home last night when suddenly she _____ the ice crack. (skate, hear)　Before she could react, she already _____ through the ice. (fall)　Fortunately, her skating partner, Hans Dekker, _____ about a hundred feet ahead of her when she _____ . (skate, fall)　He _____ her cries, _____ back to her, and _____ her to safety. (hear, skate, pull)

Both Van Dine and Dekker _____ on the pond many times before without incident. (skate)

6 **Close-up**

SENSE VERBS WITH BASE AND PROGRESSIVE FORMS OF VERBS

	saw	the water	rising.
I	heard	my friend	scream.
	felt	my heart	pounding.

Use the base form of the verb to describe a momentary or completed action. Use the progressive form to describe a continuous action. Compare: I heard Tom *call* my name. "Anne!" I heard Tom *calling* my name. "Anne, Anne, Anne!"

7 TELL A STORY

Rewrite the following account of a fire, using sense verbs as in *Close-up 6*. Change as many sentences as you can.

I was lying in bed . . . when all of a sudden I heard . . .

Eyewitness account!

I was lying in bed taking a nap last week when all of a sudden someone in the hall yelled, "Fire!" I got up quickly and opened my door. Smoke was pouring out of the apartment next door. The hall was getting warmer. Just then, the fire alarm went off. My heart was pounding as I raced down the stairs two at a time. Other people were running down the stairs ahead of me. When I got outside, I experienced a great sense of relief. A cool breeze was blowing across my face. A few minutes later, fire trucks pulled up in front of the building.

8 TELL A STORY

First, complete the story about the hiker. Then choose one of the headlines below, or write one of your own, and write a short article to go with it. You may want to connect your ideas with some of the expressions in the box.

when	just then	a few minutes later
as soon as	suddenly	finally
right after	all of a sudden	

Some headlines

Mountain Climber Stranded on Peak for Two Days
Woman Gets 'Surprise of Her Life'
Brothers Reunited After 40 Years
'I Still Can't Believe It'
Couple Lives Out Lifelong Dream

Hiker Thought His End Had Come

John Cunningham, 42, returned home safely last night after two terrifying hours in Rosewood Park. Cunningham had spent a pleasant morning in the park without incident. His problems began when he decided to leave the hiking trail and look around on his own. "I was just walking along," Cunningham told reporters, "when all of a sudden I heard someone scream. Just then . . ."

Your turn

1.

The people in the photos have all been in the news because of their exciting and sometimes dangerous activities. Look at the photos and captions. Then, working in groups, try to fill in the details of these events. Consider each of these questions:

1. What took place from the beginning of the event to the end?
2. What did the person in the photo tell reporters? What reasons did he or she give for choosing this activity?
3. Were people watching? What were their opinions?
4. What happened to the person in the photo after the event?

2. Listen in 📼

Two people are talking in front of the World Trade Center in New York City. Read the statements below. Then listen to the conversation and say *Right* or *Wrong*. Correct the wrong statements.

1. In the summer of 1974, the woman had a job near the World Trade Center.
2. When the woman got to the World Trade Center, she saw Petit walking across a tightrope.
3. The police cheered Petit after the event and didn't arrest him.
4. According to Petit, he walked across the tightrope because he wanted fame and money.

3.

Have you ever done anything really dangerous just for the excitement of it? Tell a group of students about your experience.

4. On your own

Write a short news story, choosing one of the topics below.

1. You are a reporter who witnessed one of the activities in the photos. Write an account of it. Make sure to include a headline for your story.
2. A local magazine has heard about the experience you described to your group in exercise 3 and has asked you to write a story about it. Your story must be 400 words or less. Include a suggested headline.

Mark Gottleib playing the violin in a water tank with sharks in it, San Francisco, summer of 1979.

Knievel jumping over nine cars at a daredevil show, Madison Square Garden, New York City, July 9, 1971.

Evel Knievel in his rocket as it falls into the Snake River Canyon in Twin Falls, Idaho, September 8, 1974. He had tried to fly across the entire canyon, but failed.

Philippe Petit walking across a tightrope between the towers of the World Trade Center, New York City, August 7, 1974.

Stacy Chanin swimming around Manhattan Island, August 29, 1984.

The Mysterious Gift of the Prodigy

by Roderick MacLeish

Felix Mendelssohn as a young conductor.

Wolfgang Amadeus Mozart will be remembered as one of history's most famous child prodigies. By the age of eight, he had performed in half the great cities of Europe and was about to write his first three symphonies. He died shortly before his 36th birthday, but the world recognizes him as one of the finest composers who ever lived.

For centuries, people have been amazed by children of unusual talent. Pianist and composer Felix Mendelssohn had composed a fair amount of music by the time he was 11. His fourth opera was produced in Berlin when he was only 18. John Stuart Mill, the 19th-century British philosopher, read Greek at three and had worked his way through elementary geometry and algebra and a large body of literature and history by the time he was 12.

Success has not always brought happiness to prodigies. When he was 20, John Stuart Mill suffered a serious mental crisis. "I seemed to have nothing left to live for," he wrote years later. Other well-known prodigies have had similar experiences.

A number of history's most famous prodigies had something else in common: they did not live very long lives. Composer Franz Schubert died at 31. Scientist Blaise Pascal died before he was 40.

Those who have studied today's prodigies closely have observed that they live under the great weight of their loneliness. In school with children their own age, they become bored, frustrated, and may simply turn off learning completely. Ten-year-old geniuses, if sent to universities because of their mental abilities, can't fit in. Emotionally, they're still children.

Many children, as they enter adolescence, begin to turn to other teenagers for affection, encouragement, and a sense of belonging. This can be a very difficult time in the lives of prodigies. They know they're different, and other teenagers know it, too.

"I'm afraid of not having any friends," says Mac Randall. Mac, 11, taught himself to use an electric typewriter at the age of three. At four, he began to write horror stories. He recently wrote a rock opera.

Even though there has been a fascination with child prodigies for centuries, there has been little serious study of them until recently. Some surprising common characteristics have been identified. The vast majority are boys. They are usually first-born children of middle-class families. Often, their parents are past the usual child-bearing age. Many are born by Caesarean section rather than by natural childbirth. They often have parents who seem to be trying to realize their own ambitions through their amazing children. And prodigies usually have a strange sense of humor.

Although a child may be born with outstanding genetic potential, this potential will not necessarily develop. "Just having the gene is not enough," says Harvard University psychologist Howard Gardner. Something in the environment must nourish the potential.

And although many prodigies enjoy the satisfaction of extraordinary achievement, public praise, and material wealth, even the most successful sometimes question the value of their lives and accomplishments. "I have a longing which grows stronger as I get older," confesses the acclaimed American concert pianist Eugene Istomin, "to be mediocre."

Figure it out

1. A prodigy is a child with unusual ability. Before you read the article, try to decide which of these statements a prodigy might make. Say *Right* or *Wrong* for each statement below. When you have finished reading, correct your answers.

1. I have already done a lot, and there's nothing much left for me to do.
2. My classmates don't like me.
3. I never feel alone.
4. My parents are younger then most of my friends' parents.
5. I often laugh about things that aren't funny to other children.
6. I want to be just like everyone else.
7. My parents don't encourage me to succeed.
8. I've never made any money.

2. Which of these topics does the article discuss? Say *Yes* or *No*. If your answer is *Yes*, support it with at least one fact from the article.

1. the short lives of some famous prodigies
2. the emotional problems of prodigies
3. some famous women prodigies
4. the personal life of Mozart
5. some characteristics that prodigies have in common with each other

3. Many adjectives can be changed into nouns by adding the suffix *-ness*. Complete the paragraph with appropriate nouns from the list. There is more than one possible way to complete it.

closeness   loneliness
friendliness   sadness
happiness   strangeness

Ruby was a child prodigy. She remembers the _____ she felt as a teenager when she had no friends. Ruby had talent and money, but she couldn't find _____ . Her parents thought they could see the _____ in her eyes.

Sometimes I wish . . .

Try this

Is there something in your life you're trying to make a decision about, such as choosing a field of study or a career, changing jobs, finding a place to live, getting married, or maybe just buying something? Tell another student about it and explain why you're undecided.

John Walsh is tutoring Luke Bennett in math.

● Luke Bennett
○ John Walsh

● I just hope I pass the test on Monday. Let's face it, John, I'm no genius like you are.
○ I wish you wouldn't call me a genius.
● Listen, any fifteen-year-old who's graduating from high school . . .
○ I'm tired of everyone talking about it all the time, though.
● Oh, they're just jealous of you because you have no problems in school, so they try to make you feel really different from everyone.
○ You know, you might find this hard to believe, but sometimes I wish I were worried about passing the math test like everyone else. I really envy you.

● Why would *you* envy *me*? Because I have trouble in math?
○ Well, because you're on the soccer team, for instance . . .
● Listen, I just got an idea. Since we don't have to work on my math after the test on Monday, why don't we work on your soccer? You can come over to my house after school.
○ I don't know, Luke. I'm terrible at soccer.
● That may be . . .
○ How come you want me to come over then?
● Because I kind of like you, even though I'm jealous of you, too.

Figure it out

Match.

1. How come   a. you want me to come over?
2. Why   b. do you want me to come over?

3. I hope   a. I did better in math.
4. I wish   b. I do well in math.

5. You're smart   a. so they're jealous of you.
6. You're lonely   b. but they're jealous of you.

7. I envy him   a. even though he's got a lot of money.
8. I feel sorry for him b. because he's got a lot of money.

Ways to say it

ASK FOR AN EXPLANATION

Complete the sentences. Another student will ask you for an explanation about some of them.

- How come you've decided to stop taking English?
- ○ Well, I'd really like to continue taking it, but I'm too busy this month, so I think I'll wait until next semester.

1. I've decided to _____ .
2. I never learned to _____ .
3. I couldn't go to _____ .
4. I won't be able to _____ .
5. I've always wanted to _____

> *How come . . . ?* is informal.
>
> Compare the formation of sentences with *How come . . . ?* and *Why . . . ?*:
> How come *you don't* speak English?
> Why *don't you* speak English?

2 **GIVE AN EXPLANATION**

Explain to another student why you like or dislike something, using *even though*, *although*, or *though*.

- I hear you just moved into a new apartment.
- ○ Yes. I'm really happy about it, even though I'm paying a much higher rent.

Some topics
your (new) apartment
your (new) job
a class you're taking
the city or town you live in
a certain sport or hobby

I'm really happy about my new apartment, even though I'm paying a much higher rent.

I'm a guidance counselor. Although my work is sometimes frustrating, I feel I can make a difference in people's lives.

I'm very happy with this English class. I don't have enough time to study, though.

3 **GIVE REASONS**

Have conversations with another student that include the sentences below with *since*.

- Since it's such a beautiful day, why don't we do something outdoors?
- ○ That's a good idea. Maybe we could go for a walk on the beach....

1. Since it's such a beautiful day, MAKE A SUGGESTION .
2. Since you're not doing anything Friday, EXTEND AN INVITATION .
3. TELL ABOUT A FUTURE PLAN , since I have the money and the time.
4. TELL ABOUT A PAST EVENT , since I had no money and no time.
5. Since _____ , PERSUADE SOMEONE TO DO SOMETHING .

My new apartment is bigger,	so	I like it.

◄ It's bigger. *As a result*, I like it.

I like my new apartment	because	it's bigger.

◄ *The reason* I like it is that it's bigger.

Since	I like my new apartment, I'm willing to pay more.

◄ *Given the fact that* I like it, I'm willing to pay more.

I like my new apartment,	even though / although	the rent is higher.

◄ The rent is higher. *But I still* like it.

I like my new apartment.	The rent is higher,	though.

◄ I like it, *but* the rent is higher.

So and *though* are informal. *Although* is more formal than *even though* and is more often used in writing.

Because is used to give a reason. *Since* is often used to refer to a reason already given:

● John didn't study for the test.
○ Well, *since* he didn't study, he probably won't do well.

---

5 GIVE REASONS

These letters will be better if more conjunctions are used. Rewrite the formal letter, using two different conjunctions taught in *Close-up 4*. Rewrite the informal letter, using three different conjunctions.

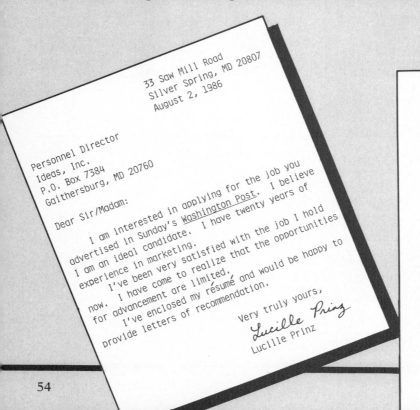

33 Saw Mill Road
Silver Spring, MD 20807
August 2, 1986

Personnel Director
Ideas, Inc.
P.O. Box 7384
Gaithersburg, MD 20760

Dear Sir/Madam:

I am interested in applying for the job you advertised in Sunday's <u>Washington Post</u>. I believe I am an ideal candidate. I have twenty years of experience in marketing.

I've been very satisfied with the job I hold now. I have come to realize that the opportunities for advancement are limited.

I've enclosed my résumé and would be happy to provide letters of recommendation.

Very truly yours,
Lucille Prinz
Lucille Prinz

September 29, 1986

Dear Judy,

Sorry I've been out of touch for so long. I've been looking for a new job. I haven't had much time for anything else. In some ways I really like the job I have, and the people are very nice. The work has become boring. Believe it or not, I'm already sad about leaving. I haven't even found a new job yet!

Ted called me when he was in town on business. He was really busy. We never got together.

6 *HOPE* VS. *WISH:* PRESENT AND FUTURE TIME

Hopes and wishes about the present

> I hope Joan *isn't* sick. (She might be.)
> I wish Joan *weren't* sick. (She is.)

Hopes and wishes about the future

> I hope I *can take* some time off next week. (I might be able to.)
> I wish I *could take* some time off next week. (I can't.)

> I hope my boss *will give* me a raise. (He or she might.)
> I wish my boss *would give* me a raise. (He or she won't.)

Use *hope* when you're talking about something that's possible. Use *wish* when you're talking about something that's contrary-to-fact.

When it refers to the future, the verb following *hope* is often in the present tense. Compare the meaning of these sentences:

I hope I *pass* the test. (I haven't taken it yet.)

I hope I *passed* the test. (I've taken it, but I haven't gotten the results.)

Hopes and wishes about the past will be covered in Unit 15.

7 TALK ABOUT HOPES AND WISHES

Read about these people and say what they hope and wish.

1. Bridget is worried about her son who's away at school. He hardly ever calls, and she can't get in touch with him.
   Bridget hopes _____ .
   She wishes _____ .

2. Anna is working against a deadline to finish a project. She doesn't think there are enough hours in the day to do the work, though.
   Anna hopes _____ .
   She wishes _____ .

3. Nina just moved to the United States and is looking for a job. Since she's not fluent in English, she's signed up for an English class.
   Nina hopes _____ .
   She wishes _____ .

4. Michael is an artist. He's worried about paying his rent this month because he can't make a living selling his paintings.
   Michael hopes _____ .
   He wishes _____ .

8 TALK ABOUT HOPES AND WISHES

Write a short paragraph about yourself that is similar to the items in exercise 7. End it with a hope and a wish.

55

Your turn

1.

All of the couples mentioned have had to make decisions about the education of their children. What explanations can you give for why they made the choices they did? Do you agree with their decisions? Work in groups to discuss these questions.

Juan and Luisa Rosada's son, Rafael, was a concert pianist at the age of ten. He loved the piano and practiced at least five hours a day. Now Rafael is fourteen and he doesn't want to play anymore. The Rosadas do not seem upset and are not pushing him. Rafael was supposed to go to a private music school next year, but the Rosadas have now enrolled him in the local public school.

Lucy and Bob Clinton's daughter, Amy, is a child actress. Lucy Clinton started taking her daughter to auditions for TV commercials when she was three years old. Now Amy is ten and she spends almost all her free time in TV studios. Amy would rather stay home and play with her friends, but her parents don't want her to give up acting.

Lou and Sally Turner have two teenage children, Diane and Greg. Even though the Turners have the money, they want their children to pay for their own college education. Diane and Greg work three days a week after school in a local grocery store, baby-sit evenings and weekends, and have full-time summer jobs.

Nathan and Wendy Miller's children are also teenagers. The Millers do not want their children to work and are doing everything possible to pay for their education. The Millers do not have much money and have taken on extra jobs so that their children can go to college.

Luke and Kathy McNally have an eight-year-old son, Bobby. Bobby's teacher feels that Bobby learns more quickly than his classmates. The school has suggested moving Bobby to the next grade, but his parents have refused. Instead, the McNallys have convinced the school to let Bobby tutor a few of his classmates, and they are encouraging him to get more involved in after-school activities.

Marcy and Bill Randall have a nine-year-old daughter, Laura, whose situation was very similar to Bobby's. The Randalls had their daughter moved from the fourth to the fifth grade. Laura has had a little trouble making friends because she is at least a year younger than all of her classmates. She finds her schoolwork very challenging, though.

2. Listen in 📼

Luke and Kathy McNally are being interviewed on the radio program, *Educational Viewpoint*. Read the question below. Then listen to a short part of that program and choose *a*, *b*, or *c*.

Which of these sentences best summarizes the McNallys' point of view?
a. Skipping a grade won't make school interesting.
b. Teaching a child to be a good person is just as important as teaching him or her academic skills.
c. Children who skip grades are usually unhappy.

3. On your own

Write a letter, choosing one of the topics below.

1. You've spent a lot of time this week thinking about your child's (or children's) future. Write a personal letter to a relative, explaining a decision you've made. You may play the role of a parent you've discussed or write about your own child(ren).
2. Write a personal or business letter, giving as many reasons as you can for any sort of decision you've made recently.

THOUGHTS WHILE FALLING 1,000 FEET TO THE SEA

MIDLAND, Mich., Aug. 25, 1982— As the airplane plunged 1,000 feet toward the icy water above the Arctic Circle, Ann Sinclair said she "just sat down and watched," silent, scared, and never expecting to live.

"The odds were about a million to one," she said. "We weren't supposed to live."

Miss Sinclair, 24 years old, a native of Midland, is visiting her parents this week after an oil company ship rescued her and five others from the water off northwestern Canada a week ago.

The twin-engine propeller plane crashed near Tukoyaktuk, above the Arctic Ocean, on Miss Sinclair's first assignment for the National Oceanic and Atmospheric Administration. Traveling with three other scientists, a pilot, and a copilot, she was sent to the area to observe Bowhead whales, an endangered species.

Their plane was 17 miles from its base at 1,000 feet when both engines died.

"It's funny, because . . . your instincts take over," she said. "I don't know what I was thinking. I never put on my seat belt. I just sat down and watched."

As the plane fell toward the water, survival suits were distributed.

"The pilot brought the plane down to 10 feet, then turned it into the wind so it stalled and dropped," Miss Sinclair said. "The pilot was so good the impact wasn't as bad as it could have been, but it's like hitting a brick wall at 30 miles an hour.

The only thing that saved us was the pilot's turning into the wind like that. He saved our lives."

Shortly before the crash, Miss Sinclair said she heard the pilot radio the position of the plane. After the plane hit the water, the passengers made their escape.

The process was slowed, however, when one of the scientists grabbed the handle of the emergency exit door and it came off in his hand. The crew and passengers finally got out through the front door of the plane, taking with them a life raft that had been placed on board only the night before.

Miss Sinclair said a lifelong bond has developed between her and the five others who went down.

"I'm so proud of this team," she said. "Everyone just moved. There was no room for emotion. No one panicked."

Miss Sinclair's agency has given her two weeks to recover from her experience, but she does not believe she will use it.

"I just think it's important to get back on the horse," she said.

As you read the article, pay attention to the sequence of events. Then, when you have finished, put the events below in *reverse* order, listing the most recent first. Using the past perfect, write a paragraph describing the events that led up to Ann Sinclair's rescue.

Start like this:
On August 19, 1984, an oil company ship rescued Ann Sinclair and five others from the water off northwestern Canada.

End like this:
The agency is giving her two weeks to recover from the experience.

___ Terrified, Miss Sinclair watched the plane fall toward the icy water minutes before the crash.
___ Only seventeen miles from its base, the plane suddenly developed engine trouble.
___ The National Oceanic and Atmospheric Administration sent Miss Sinclair to the Arctic to study Bowhead whales.
___ Their plane crashed near the Arctic Circle.

Review (8)

2 Put the verbs in parentheses into the simple past, the past continuous, or the past perfect.

One fateful day in August, Ann Sinclair _____ over the Arctic Ocean. (fly)   To Ann's horror, both engines of the plane suddenly _____ when the plane _____ to its base. (fail, return)   Fortunately, everyone _____ onto a life raft. (escape)   After the plane _____ 1,000 feet and _____ into the icy water, the passengers and crew _____ for an hour on the raft. (fall, crash, wait)   Finally, a ship _____ Miss Sinclair and the five other people who _____ aboard the plane. (rescue, be)

3 Rewrite this description of an earthquake, using sense verbs as in the example. Change as many sentences as you can.

One evening I was at a party in a friend's apartment when I felt the walls and floor start to shake....

```
              The Worst Experience of My Life

     One evening I was at a party in a friend's apartment when the walls
and floor started to shake.  Things fell from the bookshelves and tables.
Then someone screamed, "Earthquake!"  My hands and face went cold.
Another person passed out.

     The apartment was on the fourteenth floor of the building, and the
hall was crowded with people.  Someone was pushing me.  A few people fell
on the stairs.  There was smoke and the fire alarm went off.  I was so
relieved when the cold air touched my face!
```

4 Bruce, who was at the party, is telling his friend Martha about the earthquake. Rewrite Bruce's description, changing the sentences in brackets to ones with *so* or *such* and a result clause.

Martha: I read there was an earthquake while I was away. Was it bad?

Bruce: [Yes, it was a very bad earthquake, and it destroyed several buildings.]

Martha: Where were you when it happened?

Bruce: I was at a party. I didn't get too nervous, but [one person was very frightened, and he fainted.] It seemed like hours before we got outside. [There were a lot of people, so we couldn't move very quickly.] When I finally got outside, [it was a great relief, and *I* almost fainted.]

5 Read the statements below. Then listen to one side of a conversation about a hurricane. Each time you hear a pause, choose the appropriate response, *a* or *b*.

1. a. What a frightening experience that must have been!
   b. How disappointing!

2. a. I would have panicked!
   b. How depressing!

3. a. How embarrassing!
   b. I would have been terrified!

59

Bickering employees are bad news in the office

by Beth Brophy

If you've ever spent time with a bickering couple, you can sympathize with managers who supervise two bickering employees.

"It's destructive if two people are arguing," said Marilyn Moats Kennedy, managing partner of Career Strategies in Wilmette, Illinois.

It hurts productivity, keeps the manager from other things, and often other employees spend time listening to it, so you're losing their time, too, Kennedy says.

As long as the problem employees have jobs that aren't related, separating them is the simplest solution, says Allan Cohen, management professor at Babson College and senior vice president of consulting firm Goodmeasure Inc. in Boston.

But putting up fences won't work if job duties overlap. In that case, the manager must make them cooperate. "If two secretaries won't cooperate and answer each other's phones, I'll bang their heads together," Kennedy said.

Surprisingly, experts say the cause of the problem often lies within the company's structure.

"What looks like personality conflicts could be natural, based on organizational structure," Cohen said.

In a rivalry between sales and production managers, the salesperson might want many varieties of a product manufactured to satisfy customers; the production manager might want to manufacture one product to keep costs down. If two salespeople are fighting over customers, the organizational structure may encourage nasty competition, Cohen says.

Perhaps the employees who don't get along should report to separate people so they're not trying to get the same boss's time and attention, says Richard Miners, a partner at the management consulting firm of Goodrich & Sherwood in New York.

"Or maybe there's a communication problem, and only one person gets his or her words in and the other feels like a stepchild," Miners said.

The solution: The manager should make sure the company's reward system and division of jobs isn't creating the behavior problem.

"That's the case more often than personality," Cohen said.

Of course, sometimes there is a true personality conflict that the manager can't ignore.

In that case, "Bring both parties together and leave the room," said workplace psychologist Marilyn Machlowitz. "Don't attempt to mediate or you'll be the common enemy."

Warn both parties that if they don't begin to cooperate professionally, a lot is at stake, ranging from a transfer to unemployment. "Often one or both has to go," Machlowitz said, "because the work is not getting done...."

As you read the article, pay attention to the opinions in it. You may wish to make a list. Then, when you have finished, say *Right* or *Wrong* for each statement below. Correct the wrong statements.

1. Even if bickering employees share duties, the manager should separate them so they don't have to work near each other.
2. Bickering on the job is not always caused by personality conflicts.
3. If two employees with a personality conflict are bickering, the boss should be present to solve the problem.
4. It is natural for employees to bicker when the structure of the organization encourages competition.
5. If bickering employees don't have to share duties, sometimes a solution is to give them different bosses.

2 These are some conversations taking place in an office. Combine the sentences in brackets, using *so*, *because*, *since*, *even though*, *although*, or *though*. Some items have more than one answer.

1. ● I've noticed the two of you haven't been getting along. [You may not always agree. You still have to work together.]
   ○ We know. We'll try our best to improve.

2. ● Julia is never at work on time. [She's always late. She missed the important meeting yesterday.]
   ○ [You're going to have to talk to her. This really can't continue.]

3. ● Two of my employees don't get along. Do you think I should talk to them?
   ○ I would if I were you. [They both work for you. Their problem is your problem, too.]

4. ● I think you should consider firing Kevin Wells. He can't seem to get along with anyone.
   ○ [I know he's hurting productivity. I'd still like to keep him.] I think he has talent.

3 Some employees at a company are talking about their bosses. Put the verbs in parentheses into the simple present, the present continuous, or the past tense, using the frequency adverbs when they are given. Pay careful attention to the attitude of the speaker. When the attitude is negative, there are two possible answers.

1. My boss _____ his mind about everything. (always change) First he _____ me to write a ten-minute speech, and then he suddenly _____ me to speak for twenty minutes. (tell, want)

2. My boss gives me a lot of responsibility. First she _____ me how to do all the research for a new project, and then she _____ me the entire project. (teach, assign) Sometimes the responsibility makes me nervous, but she _____ me useful advice. (always give)

3. My boss is very easygoing and generous. First he _____ for my dinner last night, and then he even _____ me ten dollars to take a taxi home. (pay, lend) He _____ me with everything. (always help)

4. My boss drives me crazy. She _____ over my shoulder. (always look) Not only that, she _____ to my telephone calls. (always listen) If things don't change, I'm going to have to look for a new job.

4 The office manager is talking to two problem employees. Complete what the manager says, filling in each blank with a form of *must* or *have to* and a form of the verb in parentheses. Make sure to use the correct tense. Some items have two answers.

This bickering on the job _____ . (continue) Yesterday I _____ working twice to talk to you. (stop) Everyone in this office _____ at least an hour because they were listening to you instead of working. (waste) You both have good jobs here, but you _____ to keep them. (want) You _____ your differences right away. (settle) You _____ on everything, but you _____ with each other. (agree, cooperate)

Vietnamese Refugees Settle in Chicago

by Marilyn Balamaci

It's a typical day along Chicago's Argyle Street. Shoppers are buying groceries, clothing, and videotapes.

Among the products along the four-block-long commercial district are *muoc mam*, a fish sauce (pronounced *nuk mum*); *ao dai*, a long dress (pronounced *owl zye*); and the fastest-selling video, *Kung Fu*.

This is Vietnam, Chicago-style, where an estimated 7,000 refugees live and shop.

Within a crowded area of Chicago's Uptown-Edgewater section lies perhaps the USA's most diverse community. Along with the Vietnamese are blacks, Cambodians, Chinese, Laotians, Hmongs, Thais, Appalachian whites, Hispanics, and Native Americans.

Since the first wave of refugees in 1975, after the fall of Saigon, the Vietnamese have established 35 businesses here.

"The Vietnamese community has added a new dimension to our neighborhood," said Alderman Marion Volini. "They are high achievers in school."

On weekends, other Vietnamese come from surrounding states to shop. They may visit a video store, gift shop, jewelry store, insurance office, pharmacy, and doctor's office.

"I like to come here shopping," said Lien Lam, a Lansing, Michigan, bank teller who bought spices, rice, and vegetables. "We can get the feeling we are home."

Physician Lang Tran knows how to make his patients feel welcome. He plays a Chinese video love story for waiting clients.

Business is good. Tran said that while in Chicago there is one doctor for every 500 residents, he and the other two doctors on Argyle Street have 20,000 potential patients.

The Vietnamese are not only waiting for doctors, but for citizenship. Of the 17,000 Vietnamese in the state, an estimated 2,000 have become American citizens; about 12,000 have permanent resident status.

"It is a very emotional issue whether to make a commitment to stay here because they all dream of going back home," said Ngoan Le, director of the Vietnamese Community Service Center.

"Many of the refugees are here without a complete family," explained Le.

Most of the children and young adults are becoming bilingual through English as a Second Language classes. But many of the elderly do not speak English.

"The children learn the language very quickly and also adopt the American code of behavior and that runs into conflict at home," Le said.

"In general, I think the Vietnamese have adjusted well," she added. "They're the survivors."

---

1 As you read the article, try to remember interesting facts about the Vietnamese in Chicago. When you have finished, fill in the blanks with *the* or nothing. Then skim the article again to see if the facts below are correct. Say *Right* or *Wrong* for each one.

1. _____ Vietnamese community in _____ Chicago numbers around 7,000 people.
2. _____ groceries and _____ clothing from _____ Vietnam are sold in many stores along Chicago's Argyle Street.
3. _____ business is good and on weekends many Vietnamese from _____ other states come to shop.
4. Everyone who lives in _____ Chicago's Uptown-Edgewater section is from _____ Vietnam.
5. _____ Vietnamese refugees have all come to _____ United States with their families.
6. Most Vietnamese children are learning _____ English quickly in _____ classes at _____ school.

2 Liz Tran is a twelve-year-old Vietnamese refugee, and she is explaining how she learned to speak English so well. Complete the paragraph, filling in each blank with *let, make, have,* or *help*; a pronoun; and the verb in parentheses.

I started school soon after I came here, and both my friends and my teacher _____ English. (learn)   They were very patient with me and gave me confidence. There were several children from Vietnam, but my teacher never _____ Vietnamese in class. (speak)   She encouraged us to speak English, even though we made mistakes. She often _____ in small groups with children who spoke no Vietnamese. (work)

My parents _____ English, too, even though they knew very little English themselves. (learn)   They _____ every afternoon, and they only _____ TV after I had finished my homework. (study, watch)

3 Gail Adams recently moved from the United States to Rio to take a job. Complete the letter a friend wrote to her, filling in each blank with a form of one of the verbs or expressions in the list and adding the correct preposition. Some blanks have more than one answer.

be afraid   be proud   dream
be excited   be satisfied   think
be jealous   be tired   worry
be nervous

April 2, 1987

Dear Gail,

Thanks for sending me the photo you took of the children in your neighboohood. It's hard to believe you've already been in Rio for three months. I miss you a lot, and I _____ you almost every day.

I'm really happy that you _____ your new job. It sounds like a great opportunity. I admit I _____ you — it must be so exciting to live in Rio. Sometimes I _____ applying for a job overseas myself. I _____ living in California, and I'd like to try something really new and different, but I guess I _____ making a change.

Well, that's about it for now. Write when you get a chance.

Love,
Cindy

4 Imagine that you and your family have moved to a suburb of Toronto, Canada. First, complete the sentences below, using *used to, would,* or the simple past in your answers. Then use the sentences to write a short paragraph comparing the everyday life of your children to your own childhood. You may use the expressions in the box to connect your sentences.

1. We eat out a lot and, at home, we often eat frozen foods because my wife (husband) and I both work. When I was a child, my mother _____ .

2. I have to drive my children everywhere — to school, to the doctor, to visit their friends, to the movies. When I was young, _____ .

3. My children have a lot of free time, and they watch a lot of TV. When I was their age, _____ .

4. During the summer months, my children have *all* their time free. Since they don't have to go to school, the spend every day at the swimming pool. When I was growing up, _____ .

Start like this:
It's hard to believe how different from my childhood life is for my children.

End like this:
These are just a few of the differences. In general, I think these changes are good (bad) for children because . . .

Some expressions
For example, . . .
Also, . . .
Another difference is that . . .
What's more, . . .

FOCUS ON THE EFFORT, NOT THE OUTCOME'

by Marilyn Elias

Fourteen-year-old Richie Hawley had spent five years studying clarinet at the Community School of Performing Arts in Los Angeles when he was invited to try out for a concert solo with the New York Philharmonic.

Ninety-two young people were invited to the auditions; only nine won Lincoln Center solos. Hawley was among them.

The audition could have been the perfect setup for fear, worrying about mistakes, and trying to impress the judges. But Hawley says he "did pretty well at staying calm.

"And I couldn't be thinking about how many mistakes I'd make — it would distract me from playing," he says. "I don't even remember trying to impress people while I played. It's almost as if they weren't there. I just wanted to make music."

Hawley is a winner. But he didn't become a winner by concentrating on winning. He did it by concentrating on playing well.

"The important thing in the Olympic Games is not to win but to take part," said the founder of the modern Olympics, Pierre de Coubertin, 88 years ago. "The important thing in life is not the triumph but the struggle. The essential thing is not to have conquered but to have fought well."

Some people might think de Coubertin's words are naive, even self-defeating. But new research shows that his philosophy is exactly the path achievers take to win at life's challenging games.

A characteristic of high performers is their intense, pleasurable concentration on work, rather than on their competitors or future glory or money, says Dr. Charles Garfield, who has studied 1,500 achievers in business, science, sports, the arts, and professions.

"They're interested in winning, but they're most interested in self-development, testing their limits," says Garfield, president of Performance Sciences Institute in Berkeley, California, and a clinical professor at the University of California Medical School, San Francisco.

One of the most surprising things about top performers is how many losses they've had — and how much they've learned from each. "Not one of the 1,500 I studied defined losing as failing," Garfield says. "They kept calling their losses 'setbacks.'"

A healthy attitude toward setbacks is essential to winning, experts agree.

"The worst thing you can do if you've had a setback is to let yourself get stuck in a prolonged depression," says Milton Wolpin, a clinical psychologist at the University of Southern California.

Instead, Wolpin says you should analyze carefully what went wrong. Identify specific things you did right and give yourself credit for them, he says. He believes that most people don't give themselves enough praise. He even suggests keeping a diary of all the positive things you've done on the way to a goal.

Psychologist Lorraine Nadelman says parents should play games of both chance and skill with their children, and should emphasize the difference between the two.

Concentrating on the game instead of the outcome will also help you keep realistic expectations.

"A lot of people think if they win something big, it's going to make a drastic change in their lives," Wolpin says. "Then, if life settles down pretty much as before, it can leave you disappointed. Don't build up a lot of . . . unrealistic expectations."

As you read the article, pay attention to the important points that are made about winning and losing. Then, when you have finished, imagine that you started a new company and six months later it failed. Your brother agrees with the opinions in the article. Which of these statements would he make to you? Say *Right* or *Wrong*.

1. Even though you didn't succeed, you should be proud of yourself for trying.
2. Don't think of this as a "failure," but as a "setback."
3. Next time, try harder to outsmart the competition.
4. It's not smart to try something new unless you're sure you'll succeed.
5. Life is partly a game of chance; sometimes you win and sometimes you don't.
6. I'm sure you'll do well in the future because you enjoy your work so much.

2 Rewrite the paragraph, changing the parts in brackets, as in the example.

Pierre de Coubertin, the founder of the modern Olympics, said that [it was more important to take part in something than to win.] Now experts agree that [thinking about the activity itself is essential] if you want to be a winner. Contrary to popular opinion, [competing isn't a good idea.] In sports, for example, [it doesn't help you win to compete against other athletes.] [Competing against your own record is better.]

[It isn't helpful to criticize yourself too much.] [It's much more important to concentrate on your successes.] [Writing down everything you've done right is a very good idea.]

Pierre de Coubertin . . . said that taking part in something was more important than winning. Now experts agree that it's . . .

3 The members of a high-school soccer team are talking about a friendly game they're getting ready to play with another team during a community get-together. Complete the conversation, filling in the blanks with appropriate expressions from the box. Some items have two answers.

Joe: We have to win this game. We lost our last game. _____ we've never won a game with this team.

Kenny: _____ this isn't a competition. We should just play for fun.

Joe: I don't agree. _____ we're playing, we should play to win.

Paco: I agree with Kenny. I think it's more important to have a good time. I mean, _____ we lose? What's going to happen?

Joe: I really don't understand you two. When I play, I play to win. It adds excitement to the game.

besides	suppose (that)
what's more	what if
in any case	as long as
true, but	

4 Read about these people. Then complete the statements appropriately.

1. Last year Erica came in second in an all-day bicycle marathon. This year she's going to be in the marathon again.
   Erica hopes _____ .

2. Jon's basketball team is going to play an important game, but their best forward, Ned, has a sprained ankle.
   Jon and the rest of the team wish _____ .

3. Marina wants to be a research scientist, but her parents can't afford to send her to college. She's entered a competition for a scholarship.
   Marina hopes _____ .

4. Roberto's soccer team is going to have a game this afternoon. The game was supposed to be yesterday, but it rained all day.
   Roberto hopes _____ .

5. Christos is an actor, and there's going to be an important audition next Tuesday. They won't postpone the audition, even though Christos will be in Mexico on vacation next week.
   Christos wishes _____ .

6. Jenny likes to play team sports. The problem is she isn't very athletic.
   Jenny wishes _____ .

LASERS

The Light of the Twenty-first Century

A scientific principle is often understood long before someone is able to put it to use. For example, people knew of the power of steam before there were any steam engines. But sometimes they take place at the same time — a new scientific principle and a new invention. This was the case a little more than twenty years ago with a device called the laser. To many people, lasers were very mysterious.

The word *laser* stands for Light Amplification by Stimulated Emission of Radiation. More simply, a laser is a device that produces a very strong light. The light from a laser is called *coherent* light. The light we are most familiar with is *incoherent* light. Incoherent light comes from electric light bulbs and the sun. This light moves in all directions. The light from a laser, however, moves in only one direction and is much stronger.

Laser light is created by a process called *stimulated emission*. In this process, the atoms of a certain substance, such as a crystal or gas, are excited in such a way that they produce an extremely strong light that travels in one direction. A person working with a laser can aim this light in any direction. This light is called a *laser beam*.

Once laser light was developed, scientists immediately started to think about its applications. One of the laser's earliest uses was to measure distances and speeds. It was discovered that this could be done with amazing accuracy. For example, the distance to the moon was measured to within a foot, and the exact speed of light was determined to be 186,282.397 miles per second.

In its early days, the military also thought about using the laser. The laser was capable of "selective" destruction as opposed to total nuclear war, which would have disastrous results.

But research into constructive (positive) uses of the laser has taken place just as quickly. The laser can be used in surgery. This marvelous device can open and close an incision without the danger of infection. A laser beam can be used in delicate eye operations. For example, it can be used to reattach a retina, and it can prevent excessive bleeding of tiny blood vessels in the eye.

The laser is also important in the study and treatment of cancer. A laser beam can remove a cancerous growth and completely destroy it. No dangerous cancer cells are left behind which might spread to other parts of the body. Because a laser can concentrate on an individual cell, and even a part of a cell, it could become a tool for studying and preventing this deadly disease.

Lasers are used for everyday tasks as well. In factories, they are used to cut cloth, harden metals, and — with robots — increase the accuracy of work on assembly lines. In supermarkets, a laser at the checkout counter reads the price codes on packages. These codes consist of closely-spaced black lines. The information is put into the cash register, which then records it as a price on a receipt.

The laser promises to bring great changes in the way telephones work. In ordinary telephone technology, sound waves travel along thousands of miles of copper wire. But a laser can transmit sound waves much faster. In addition, the laser would lessen the need for copper, a natural resource.

The laser is also used in video disc players to show programs on television. When a disc is inserted into the player, the laser can "read" the information on it in order to produce the sound and picture on the TV.

There are thousands of uses for laser light, but they are only a beginning. The laser could truly become the light of the twenty-first century.

A GTE technician watching laser crystals grow.

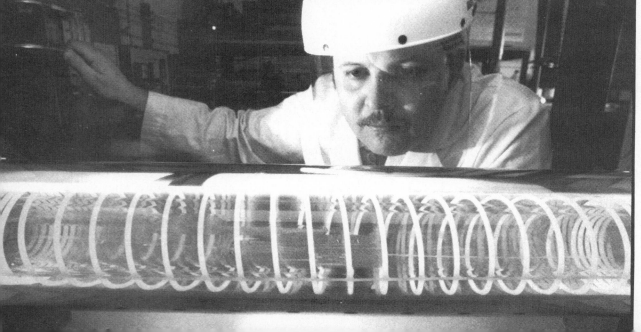

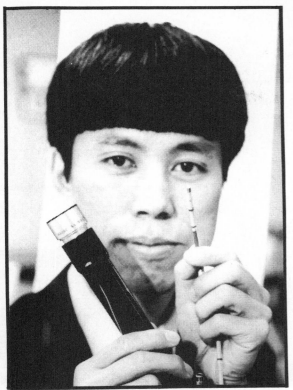

A laser used to treat heart attack patients.

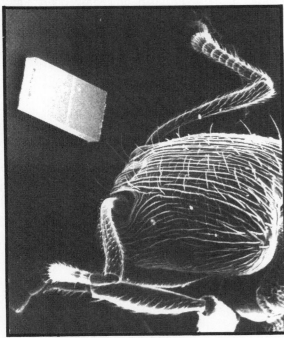

GTE's laser transmitter next to the head of an ant.

MACARONI & CHEESE DINNER

0   7 1923 98118

A laser price code.

Figure it out

1. **Before starting to read, look at the photos and the title of the article. What do you think the article is about? When you have finished reading, correct your answer if necessary.**

2. **Read the first three paragraphs. Then explain in your own words what a *laser beam* is.**

3. **As you read, pay attention to the different ways lasers are used. When you have finished, give at least three uses of lasers. Then look back at the article and explain in more detail what the laser can do in each case.**

4. **Match.**

1. produce	a. send
2. application	b. cut
3. device	c. use
4. transmit	d. instrument
5. incision	e. create

5. **The suffix *-ous* means "possessing or having" and changes a noun into an adjective, as in *cancerous*—"possessing or having cancer." Complete the paragraph, filling in each blank with an appropriate word from the list.**

cancerous	humorous	mysterious
dangerous	marvelous	numerous

About twenty years ago, a laser was a new and _____ device. Now it is clear that laser light has _____ applications. For example, it can remove a _____ growth and prevent its _____ spread to other parts of the body. This _____ device may truly become the light of the twenty-first century.

It's not ready yet.

Have you ever purchased something expensive, such as a stereo or a television, that didn't work properly? What did you do about it? Tell another student about your experience.

- ● Receptionist
- ○ Jeff Roberts
- ▲ Annette Solano

Jeff Roberts wants to know if his video disc player has been repaired yet. 🔲

- ● Good morning, Supertronix Stereo.
- ○ Repair department, please.
- ● Just a minute, please.... (*Rrring, rrring*)
- ▲ Repair department.
- ○ Hello. I'd like to know if my video disc player has been repaired yet. It's been more than three weeks....
- ▲ What's the ticket number?
- ○ Uh, let me see....It's J-5412.
- ▲ O.K., hold on.... Sorry, sir, it's not ready yet.
- ○ Not yet? It was supposed to have been ready last week. Is there some problem?

- ▲ I'm sorry, sir. The parts have been ordered, but they haven't come in yet. The laser mechanism has to be replaced, you know, and it takes a while to get that part. It looks as if it'll be another week.
- ○ Another week? I'm sorry, but something must be done about this. I want to speak to the manager.
- ▲ I *am* the manager, sir.
- ○ Oh. Well, listen . . . I brought this machine in more than three weeks ago, and I was told it would be ready in two weeks. When I called *last* week, somebody told me it would be one more week. Now I call and you tell me it's *still* not ready.
- ▲ I'm very sorry, sir. I'll call you just as soon as the repair is finished.

Figure it out

What do these sentences mean? Choose *a* or *b*.

1. I'd like to know if my video disc player has been repaired yet.
   a. I'd like to know if my video disc player is ready.
   b. I'd like to know if there's a problem with my video disc player.

2. It was supposed to have been ready last week.
   a. It must have been ready last week.
   b. It should have been ready last week.

3. Something must be done.
   a. Someone must do something.
   b. I told you to do something.

4. It looks as if it'll be another week.
   a. It will probably take a week.
   b. It will take less than a week.

68

Ways to say it

1   MAKE A COMPLAINT

**Make a phone call and complain about something you own
that has not been repaired yet. Your partner will play the role
of the mechanic.**

- ● Repair department.
- ○ Hello. I'd like to know if my stereo has been
  repaired yet.
- ● What's the ticket number?
- ○ Uh, let me see....It's 574-B.
- ● Just a minute....Sorry, ma'am, it's not ready yet.
- ○ Not yet? It was supposed to have been ready last
  week. Is there some problem?
- ● I'm sorry. The parts have been ordered, but they
  haven't come in yet.

Some appliances	
a stereo	a cassette player
a television	a microcomputer

Some ways to complain
It was supposed to have been ready last week.
I was told that it would be ready by now.
I was led to believe that it would be ready in a week.
Is there a reason why it's not ready?
Is there some problem?

Some excuses
The parts have been ordered, but they haven't come in yet.
Two of our repair people are out sick.
We're a little behind schedule at the moment.
Please be patient. We're doing the best we can.

2   MAKE A FORCEFUL COMPLAINT

Make a phone call and complain about an urgent problem. Your partner will think of a response.

- ● ...I need to speak to Mr. Tucker immediately. This is a very urgent matter.
- ○ What's the problem?
- ● I'm calling for Mrs. Cleary at 45 Hyde Street, Apartment 4D. You know, she's an elderly lady and doesn't
  feel very well. Her radiator broke two weeks ago and still hasn't been fixed. Something must be done
  immediately!
- ○ Are you sure the radiator is broken? Maybe it isn't turned on....

> Something must be done. =
> Someone must do something.

Some urgent problems
You live at 45 Hyde Street, and Mrs. Cleary, your neighbor in Apartment 4D, is an elderly lady. Her radiator broke two weeks ago and still hasn't been fixed. Call your landlord, Horace Tucker.
Your roof leaks when it rains, and it hasn't been repaired. When you got home yesterday, water was pouring into your living room. Call your landlord, Joyce Howard.
You are a surgeon and you have to perform an operation this afternoon. There's a problem with the laser surgery device. You called the manufacturer once, and someone was supposed to call you back. Call again and ask to speak to Al Chambers.

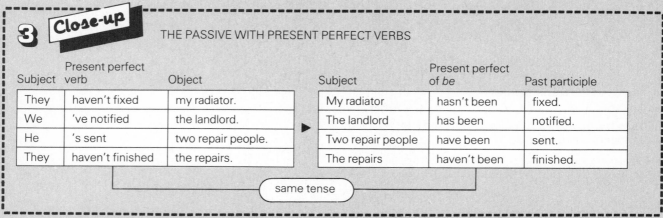

3 **Close-up** THE PASSIVE WITH PRESENT PERFECT VERBS

Subject	Present perfect verb	Object		Subject	Present perfect of *be*	Past participle
They	haven't fixed	my radiator.	▶	My radiator	hasn't been	fixed.
We	've notified	the landlord.		The landlord	has been	notified.
He	's sent	two repair people.		Two repair people	have been	sent.
They	haven't finished	the repairs.		The repairs	haven't been	finished.

same tense

4 Helen Fong has brought in her video cassette recorder (VCR) to be repaired. Look at the repair checklist form. Then, using the present perfect tense, write sentences in the passive that describe which repairs have and haven't been completed.

The recording heads have (already) been checked....

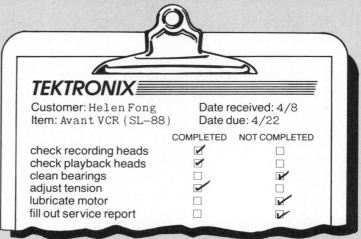

TEKTRONIX

Customer: Helen Fong   Date received: 4/8
Item: Avant VCR (SL—88)   Date due: 4/22

	COMPLETED	NOT COMPLETED
check recording heads	✓	☐
check playback heads	✓	☐
clean bearings	☐	✓
adjust tension	✓	☐
lubricate motor	☐	✓
fill out service report	☐	✓

5  STATE A PROBLEM

Play the role of a customer and describe a problem with something you own. Your partner is a mechanic and will tell you what he or she thinks is wrong with it.

- Hello, Mr. Snyder. What can I do for you?
○ I've brought my car in again. It sounds like a motorboat at full speed.
- (*A few minutes later*) Well, Mr. Snyder, it looks as [if / though] you need a new muffler.

We'll take a closer look and get back to you later today.
○ Thanks a lot.
- You bet.

Some problems
Your car sounds like a motorboat at full speed.
Your new TV isn't working right. The picture looks like a snowstorm.
You're afraid to ride your 1972 motorcycle because the engine smells like burning oil.
Your cassette player hasn't worked right for the last few days. It sounds like a thunderstorm.

Some evaluations
A customer's car most likely needs a new muffler.
A customer's new TV seems to need a new antenna.
A customer's 1972 motorcycle probably needs a tune-up.
A customer's cassette player probably needs to have the heads cleaned.

Close-up

SENSE VERBS WITH *LIKE*, *AS IF*, AND *AS THOUGH*

It	seems looks	like	a campfire.	◄	like + noun
	smells sounds	as if as though	the problem is in the engine.	◄	as if and as though + sentence

7 **Complete the conversations appropriately, using sense verbs with *like*, *as if*, or *as though* in your answers.**

1. ● Well, the elevator's not working again!
   ○ Oh, no, not again! _____ I'm really getting tired of this.

2. ● This stereo sounds terrible.
   ○ It sure does. _____ .

3. ● Something smells funny. Is it the oven?
   ○ I'm not sure, but _____ .

4. ● My car's been in the shop for repairs five times in the last three months.
   ○ _____ .

5. ● What an ugly dog!
   ○ _____ .

6. ● This soup tastes awful.
   ○ Let me try it. Ugh! _____ .

8 MAKE A COMPLAINT

Read the letter and then write a letter of complaint about an appliance you've purchased. Choose a situation from this unit or one from your own experience. You may wish to discuss the problem with another student before you begin to write.

Apartado 519
Panamá, República de Panamá
September 24, 1986

President
Astra Audio, Inc.
7789 Grove Blvd.
Palo Alto, California 94302

Dear Sir/Madam:

I am writing to you concerning an Astra stereo (Model CDP 4500) that I purchased several months ago from your dealer, Discount Stereo, here in Panama City.

From your advertisements, I was led to believe that your audio equipment was the finest that is now available. I am sorry to say that I have had problems with my stereo from the day I bought it.

The turntable does not work properly. I have brought the machine in for service twice in the last two months, and it still has not been repaired to my satisfaction. Although the service department here at Discount Stereo is willing to repair the turntable again, I feel that this should not be necessary. Please suggest a solution.

I hope you will understand my concern, and I look forward to hearing from you.

Sincerely yours,

Umberto Suárez

Your turn

1.

With a partner, act out conversations for some of these photos. Change partners after each conversation, playing Role A in half of your conversations and Role B in the other half. Here are some words you may want to use: *bug, leak* (v), *warped, bent, handle* (n), *hole, stain* (n).

Role A

You purchased one of the items in the photos. Later you discovered that something was wrong with it, or something happened to it the first time you used it. Take the item back to the appropriate store and make a complaint. Be careful not to lose your temper, and try to reach an agreement with the store.

Role B

You are the manager of a store, and a customer has come in to complain about an item in the photos. Discuss the problem with the customer and reach an agreement.

bananas

2. Listen in ▭

Two repair-shop workers at the store where the warped record was sold are now discussing stereos. Read the statements below. Then listen to the conversation and say *Right* or *Wrong*.

1. The young man wants to get rid of his Zolar stereo.
2. This store sells Zolar stereos.
3. A Zolar stereo is expensive.
4. A Uniworld stereo costs at least $500.
5. The repairman thinks Zolar is a good brand.

gloves

3. On your own

Write a letter, choosing one of the topics below.

1. You were very unhappy with the way the manager spoke to you when you complained about one of the products in the photos. Write a letter of complaint to the Better Business Bureau.
2. Write a letter of complaint about something you've had a problem with recently. You may write to an appliance store, a grocery store, a department store, your landlord, an airline, a bus company, or any other appropriate place.

a pen

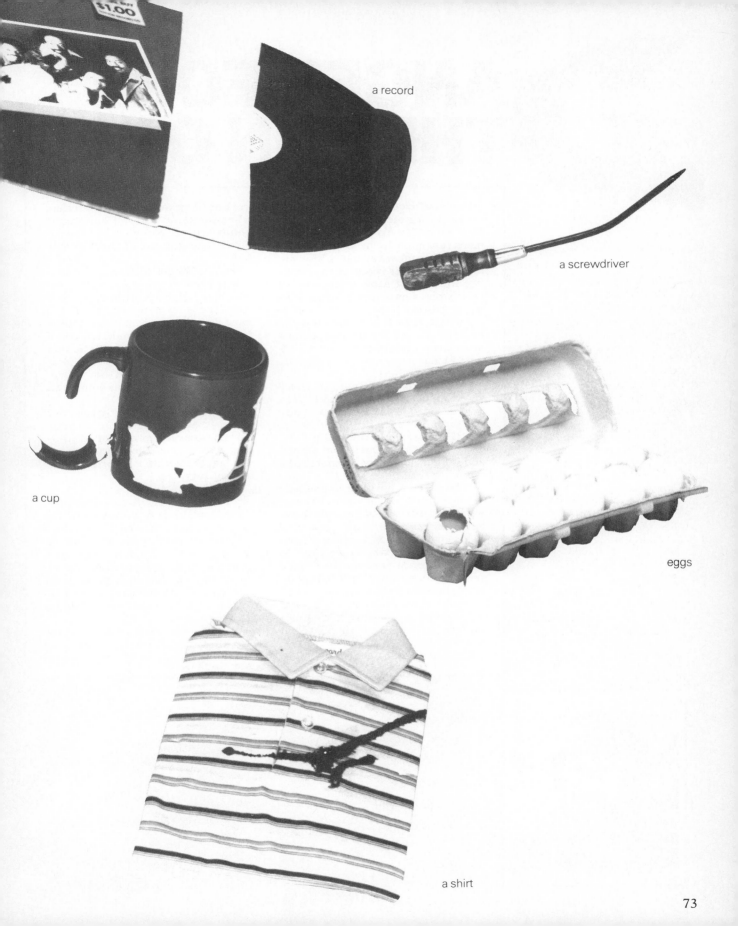

a record

a screwdriver

a cup

eggs

a shirt

73

DANGER FOR THE FUN OF IT

Dennis Joyce is a 30-year-old employee of an electric company in New York City. To put some excitement into his life, he spends many weekends and vacations white-water canoeing. He is one of the growing number of Americans who in recent years have taken up dangerous sports to fill their leisure hours.

Although he has fallen into the river several times, Mr. Joyce has never been hurt himself. Yet he admits he has seen some very serious accidents.

People who participate in risky sports usually have several things in common. Most are men. They don't like others to think of them as thrill seekers, yet they admit the dangers of their sport. And almost all of them look down on sports like tennis and golf.

"There's just nothing happening in sports like tennis and golf," said Steve Kaufman, a 44-year-old Manhattan bill collector who scuba dives in his spare time. According to him, the only people who come close to the experience of scuba divers are astronauts "because they're in a totally alien environment, too." Kaufman describes his sport as "a total isolation from anything that can interfere with your own personal sense of self."

Mr. Kaufman said his most dangerous moment as a diver came when he found himself looking at about 800 to 900 sharks. Fortunately, he got out of there really fast.

George Weigel, a 31-year-old carpenter from Pawling, New York, enjoys hang gliding. Although many risk-takers see hang gliding as the most dangerous sport of all, Weigel feels hang gliders should not be regarded as thrill seekers. Yet he said that hang gliding "scares the living daylights out of me" and that "everything else seems boring compared to it."

Why do people willingly seek out danger? According to Dr. George Serban, associate professor of clinical psychiatry at New York University, most men do it to prove their masculinity.

"The nature of the male animal is to undertake dangerous tasks and to confront them and to succeed," Dr. Serban said. When life becomes boring and routine, Serban says, and men do not have a chance for adventure or a chance to prove their masculinity, the only other possibility for them is to undertake dangerous activities.

Eric D. Rosenfeld, a 43-year-old Manhattan lawyer who has been climbing mountains for 20 years,

George Weigel

by

Judy Klemesrud

spoke of the habit-forming nature of his sport. "It's quite addictive," he says. "You get addicted to the risk factor."

In recent years, Mr. Rosenfeld has been climbing mountains in the Arctic. He contrasts the mountains in the Arctic with some in Europe. In Europe, he said, there are lines of people waiting to go up sections of mountains, guides walking around, and garbage all over the place. "In the Arctic no one's around. There's no such thing as a guide because no one's ever been there."

Although several of his friends have died while mountain climbing, Rosenfeld said, "I have an intellectual appreciation that it's risky. But I sit in my law office and tell myself that after 20 years of climbing I'm still here."

The novelty of the sport is what attracted Susan Tripp, a 35-year-old Manhattan lawyer, to skin-diving. She likes it because it "is not something many people do." That is also one of the main reasons John Wolcott, a 49-year-old printer from Edison, New Jersey, likes to go hot-air ballooning. "It makes me a hero," he said. At parties, he said, he simply introduces ballooning into the conversation, and he becomes the center of attention for at least an hour.

Figure it out

1. **Before starting to read, look at the photos and the title of the article. What do you think the article is about? Does your opinion change after you have read the first paragraph?**

2. **As you read, pay attention to the characteristics that people who like dangerous sports have in common. When you have finished, say *Right* or *Wrong* for each statement below and correct the wrong statements.**

People who participate in dangerous sports . . .
1. often don't think that they're dangerous.
2. almost always think sports like tennis and golf are boring.
3. usually are men.
4. want to feel more masculine.
5. generally don't like to talk about their sport.
6. sometimes find the sport habit-forming.

3. **The people interviewed in this article make some interesting comments. Below are some of them. Do you agree or disagree with each of them? Explain why.**

1. "There's just nothing happening in sports like tennis and golf."
2. "The nature of the male animal is to undertake dangerous tasks and to confront them and to succeed."
3. "[Participating in a dangerous sport] makes me a hero."

4. **There are many expressions in English that contain the verb *look*. Complete the paragraph with appropriate expressions from the list.**

look down on = have a bad opinion of
look up to = admire
look for = try to find
look at = see
look up = get in touch with someone *or* try to find out a fact
look over = examine quickly

Carmen Perez is the center of attention at parties. People _____ her because she goes hot-air ballooning. Carmen used to play tennis, but she started to _____ a new sport because "tennis was too boring." One day an old friend _____ Carmen, and suggested she try ballooning. Carmen loves her new sport. "I guess now I even _____ sports like tennis," she admits.

I've taken up scuba diving.

Compare some of the popular sports where you live. Which ones can be dangerous? How? Which do you like the best? Why?

Dan is talking to his friends, Linda and Toni, about his new hobby, scuba diving.

- Linda
○ Dan
▲ Toni

● I hear you've got a new hobby, Dan.
○ Yeah, I've taken up scuba diving.
● That must be a lot of fun. We should try it, Toni.
▲ Gee, I don't know about that. Isn't it kind of dangerous?
○ Well, maybe a little, but on the other hand, it's a change from working here in the store.
● Are you saying this job is boring?
○ Compared to scuba diving, it is. After all, there isn't much excitement here.
▲ Well, I was just reading about scuba diving in some magazine. Two or three percent of divers get attacked by sharks.

○ Oh, come on. You can't believe half of what you read in magazines. Do you realize that scuba diving is less risky than boating?
● Yeah. Listen, many people dive. Most of them never have any trouble.
▲ Maybe not, but *I* still think it's dangerous.
○ You know, fewer people get hurt diving than driving a car.
▲ That just can't be true.
● No, he's right. And do you know where there are even more risks than in the water or on the highway?
▲ No, where?
● Right here in the supermarket. Every day they find out that something else we eat is bad for us!

Figure it out

Fill in the blanks with *more*, *many*, or *much*.

1. _____ people enjoy scuba diving.
2. There isn't _____ danger in scuba diving.
3. _____ people get hurt driving a car than scuba diving.
4. There are _____ risks in the food we eat than on the highway.
5. _____ sports are safe if you're careful.

Ways to say it

MAKE COMPARISONS

Your partner has some reservations about a plan of yours. Support your plan by making comparisons.

● I'm thinking of taking up scuba diving. It would be exciting.

○ Isn't it kind of dangerous, though? You could get attacked by a shark.

> You could get attacked by a shark. = A shark could attack you.

> You'd like to . . .
> _____
> take up scuba diving.
> move to a big city.
> look for a job as a _____ .

● Listen, a lot more people get hurt on the highways each year than under water.

○ Well, I guess you have a point.

| Maybe so, but | I still wouldn't recommend it.
| Even so, |

Some reservations
Scuba diving could be dangerous. You could get attacked by a shark. The city is a poor place to raise children. There's a lot of crime there. _____ is a bad field to look for work in these days. There are very few opportunities/very few jobs that pay well.

Some comparisons
A lot more people get hurt on the highways each year than under water. There's less danger after dark on a busy city street than on a deserted country road. There are fewer qualified _____ now than ever before.

---

2 Close-up   QUANTIFIERS

Quantifiers with count and mass nouns

A lot of Most Many Some Not many A few Few	people	think scuba diving is exciting.

▲ count noun

A lot of Most Some Not much A little Little	exercise	is good for you.

▲ mass noun

A few and a little vs. few and little

Few and *little* emphasize the smallness of the quantity more than *a few* and *a little*. Compare:
There's *a little* excitement in baseball. (It's not that boring.)
There's *little* excitement in baseball. (It's pretty boring.)

A few and *a little* are modified by *only*, whereas *few* and *little* are modified by *very*:
Only a few people went to the game.
Very few people enjoyed themselves.

> *Many* may be used in affirmative statements. However, *much* is generally used only in negative statements.

3 Close-up

COMPARISONS WITH QUANTIFIERS

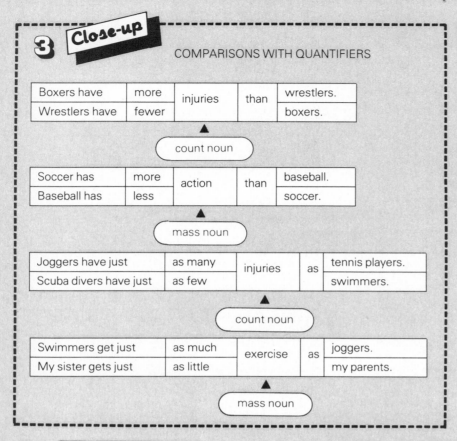

Boxers have	more	injuries	than	wrestlers.
Wrestlers have	fewer			boxers.

▲ **count noun**

Soccer has	more	action	than	baseball.
Baseball has	less			soccer.

▲ **mass noun**

Joggers have just	as many	injuries	as	tennis players.
Scuba divers have just	as few			swimmers.

▲ **count noun**

Swimmers get just	as much	exercise	as	joggers.
My sister gets just	as little			my parents.

▲ **mass noun**

4 MAKE COMPARISONS

Compare two sports. Use personal information.

- ● Do you ever play tennis?
- ○ Hardly ever. I've only played a few times. I'd rather go jogging.
- ● There isn't much excitement in jogging.
- ○ But on the other hand, you get just as much exercise and you can do it by yourself. What's more, you don't have to buy expensive equipment.
- ● What about those expensive warm-up suits?
- ○ All you really need are running shoes....

Some sports
tennis/jogging
scuba diving/hang gliding
boxing/wrestling
walking/jogging
baseball/soccer
jai alai/tennis

Some considerations
action
exercise
equipment
special clothing
expense
time
injuries
danger

5 MAKE COMPARISONS

Fill in the blanks appropriately with quantifiers or comparatives of quantifiers, using the context to figure out the answers. Some items have more than one answer.

Although _____ cities in South America get more than enough rainfall, there are _____ cities that are very dry. With the exception of southwestern Chile, which is quite wet, the southwestern part of the continent doesn't get _____ rain. If you live in Lima, Peru, for example, you can expect very _____ rain each year: the average annual rainfall is only 1.6 inches. Arica, Chile, with an average annual rainfall of only .03 inches, gets _____ precipitation _____ anywhere else in the world. _____ people alive today are old enough to remember the great drought of 1903-17, but during this period, no rain fell at all!

However, as stated above, _____ people in South America are used to rain. Asuncion, Paraguay, with an average annual rainfall of 51.8 inches, gets _____ rain in one month _____ Lima gets all year! Although Quito, Rio, and Bogota receive _____ inches of rain _____ Asuncion, all three cities still average over forty inches a year. And in tropical Suriname, the city of Paramaribo averages over ninety inches a year!

6 COMPARE OPINIONS

Give an opinion. Your partner will either agree or disagree with you.

- Auto racing must be really exciting.
- ○ Oh, I don't know about that. It's pretty dangerous.
- Maybe so, but it appeals to a lot of people. Some of them keep doing it even after they get injured.

> In informal conversation, you may form the passive with *get* rather than *be*:
>
> They *get* injured. = They *are* injured.

Some opinions
Auto racing must be really exciting. Some people keep doing it even after they get injured.
Many talented artists don't get the respect they deserve. Only a few of them make a good salary.
Most courses are too easy. Many of them are really interesting, but they're not challenging enough.
A lot of people get married too young. Many of them are very unhappy afterwards.

Some topics	
sports	school
jobs	marriage
your values (what's important to you)	

---

7 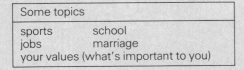 QUANTIFIERS WITH PARTITIVES

count noun

A lot of	people	I know go scuba diving.

All Many Most Some A few None	of them	have been injured.

Two	people	I know go scuba diving.

Both		have been injured.
One Neither	of them	has been injured.

mass noun

A lot of	money	is spent on sports.

All Most Some Much A little None	of it	is wasted.

---

8 MAKE COMPARISONS

What foods do you think children like where you live? Write a paragraph using quantifiers and quantifiers with partitives.

Start like this:
Most children in _____ like _____ . Many of them like _____ more than _____ . . . .

Your turn

1.

You are on a committee that is in charge of selecting sports for school athletic programs. Work in groups to compare the sports in the photos and then decide if the schools should adopt any of them. Make sure to take into account each of the considerations in the box that is part of exercise 4 on p. 78.

soccer

football

jai alai

2. Listen in 📼

Parents Against Dangerous Sports (PADS) has paid a local radio station to air their editorial. Read the paragraph below. Then listen to the editorial and fill in each blank with the correct sport.

PADS believes that _____ has no place in school athletic programs. Its members want to replace _____ with _____ . The group argues that _____ isn't as dangerous as _____ . In fact, _____ and not _____ is played in most countries.

3. On your own

Choose one of the topics below.

1. You have been selected to write the committee report on sports for school athletic programs. Compare the sports in the photos and summarize the recommendations of your group.
2. You don't approve of the sports that are taught in schools in your neighborhood. Write a letter to the appropriate person in charge, comparing the current sports with the ones you feel should replace them.

tennis

table tennis

swimming

motorcycle racing

81

HEADACHE

by MARIAN WOLBERS

When you have a headache, do you, like most people, reach for the aspirin bottle? Aspirin does reduce the pain of a headache, but you may become too dependent on it. Also, too much aspirin causes stomach bleeding and can lead to ulcers.

Here are eight natural ways to get rid of a headache:

1. Eat something soon. Preferably, eat something high in protein, a substance necessary for growth. The "hungry headache," caused by a drop in the blood-sugar supply, can be a real problem for people not eating enough at mealtimes. Why protein? Because it rebuilds your blood-sugar supply little by little. Sugary foods cause the blood sugar to go up rapidly and then drop again just as fast.

2. Wash it away. At the first sign of headache pain, get in the shower, advises Dr. Augustus S. Rose of the UCLA (University of Southern California) School of Medicine. First take a hot shower even if the pain gets worse. This will make the blood vessels open wide. Follow it immediately with a cold shower. Stay in until you shiver. Repeat this procedure if necessary. This process works well for a migraine headache. In a migraine headache, the blood vessels of the head first contract (get smaller), then dilate (open up) and press against the nerves. This pressure causes pain. Cold water makes the blood vessels contract, which eases this pressure on the nerves.

3. Freeze it out. If you are miles away from the shower, Dr. Rose suggests putting crushed ice in your mouth and throat. Again, this is useful for a migraine headache. However, this remedy is inappropriate for elderly or sick people.

4. Think it away. Sit down or lie down and close your eyes. Imagine that it is summer and you are on the beach. An ocean breeze cools your face and your hands and arms grow warmer and warmer in the hot sun. Your hands are really soaking up the sun. They become hot to the touch. Minutes pass, and when you open your eyes, you are left with very warm hands . . . and *no* headache. Thinking warmth into your hands sends blood toward them and away from the head.

5. Massage it out. Get to your head through your feet. Massaging the lower part of your big toe and the area under all your toes will lessen tension in the neck. This tension can often cause a headache.

6. Breathe it away. According to Dr. Selwyn Dexter, breathing into an ordinary paper bag can get rid of migraine headaches caused by hyperventilation. (Hyperventilation is a condition in which breathing is unusually fast or deep.) Simply breathe into a paper bag and rebreathe the same air, which is mostly carbon dioxide. This process may take as long as 15 minutes, Dr. Dexter says, but it has worked for several of his patients.

7. Press it away. Some headaches can be cured by a sensitive finger-pressure massage. The massage should be given on sensitive "trigger" points. There are three pairs of points: one at each temple, one under each shoulder blade, and a pair at the back of the neck. Press each point for 15 to 30 seconds at a time. Remember to press both points in a pair at the same time, not just one side. Doing this will help the body's natural painkillers start working. If you are alone, press the thumb of one hand against the tender spot in the "V" formed by the thumb and forefinger of the other hand.

8. Brush it away. Find a hairbrush with fairly stiff natural bristles, says biophysicist Harry C. Ehrmantraut. Then use the following procedure, first on one side of your head and then on the other: Starting a little above your temple, just above your eyebrow, brush your hair in small circles. Move the brush first up and then back before moving it down and forward to complete your circle. This way the upper part of the circle goes toward the back of the head. Then brush your hair in circles around your ear, and finally brush down to the base of your skull. After you repeat this procedure on the other side of your head, brush the hair in the center of your scalp, first on the right and then on the left. Make small circles as you start at the top of your head and move down toward the base of your skull. Brushing stimulates the skin and the tissues underneath so blood can flow more easily and more oxygen can reach the brain.

Always see a doctor for continuous or recurring head pain.

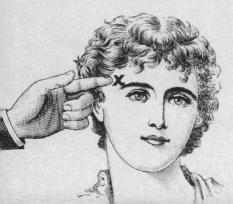  

Away

Figure it out

1. Before you read the article, make a list of some ways you have heard of to get rid of a headache. When you have finished reading, compare your list with the remedies suggested in the article. Make a new list of the remedies you think are best and save it for the future.

2. As you read, try to remember the important facts about each remedy. When you have finished, choose *a* or *b* for each statement below. Then describe in your own words the two remedies that you feel are the most practical and effective.

1. Eat something soon.
   a. Eat something high in protein.
   b. Eat something with sugar in it.

2. Wash it away.
   a. Take a very cold shower.
   b. Take a hot shower and then a cold one right after it.

3. Freeze it out.
   a. Hold ice against your forehead.
   b. Put crushed ice in your mouth and throat.

4. Think it away.
   a. Imagine that your hands are getting very warm.
   b. Imagine that your head is getting very warm.

5. Massage it out.
   a. Massage the area under your toes.
   b. Massage your neck.

6. Breathe it away.
   a. Go outside and breathe fresh air.
   b. Breathe into a paper bag.

7. Press it away.
   a. Have someone apply pressure to sensitive spots on both sides of your head.
   b. Have someone apply pressure to the side of your head that hurts the most.

8. Brush it away.
   a. Brush the back of your head near your neck.
   b. Brush both sides of your head, moving from the front to the back.

3. The words *away* and *out* are often used to form two-word verbs meaning "to get rid of something," as in *wash away* (a headache) or *freeze out* (a headache). Complete the paragraph, filling in each blank with a direct object and an appropriate two-word verb from the article. Remember that when the direct object is a pronoun it is placed between the two words.

There are many natural remedies for a headache. You can _____ by taking a shower and, if you're not near one, you can _____ with ice. People who are elderly or sick should not try to _____ , however. You can also _____ with a fairly stiff hairbrush or have a friend _____ for you with his or her fingers. If you imagine that you are lying in the hot sun, you can even _____ .

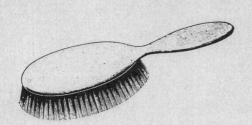

My head is killing me!

What are some situations that give you a headache? Discuss different remedies with your partner.

Dennis and Stan are postal workers. It's just before the holidays, and they're very busy.

● Dennis
○ Stan

● I don't see any more bags. All the mail must be sorted, finally. I'm dead!
○ No, I'm afraid there are two more bags left.
● Two more! My feet are ready to drop off.
○ Well, after the holidays things will slow down.
● I hope I last that long.... Something should be done about that noise outside. It's really impossible to work in here.
○ It *is* annoying. Still, it's a good thing they're fixing the sidewalk.
● They'd better fill that hole. Someone could get killed.
○ I hope they get it all done by tomorrow.

● If they don't, I'm going to go nuts.
○ Huh? Are you all right, Dennis?
● Yes, I mean, no. My head is killing me, and that noise is driving me crazy!
○ Maybe you'd better work over there in the corner.
● No, the radio is louder than the drill.
○ Look, I'll get them to turn it down.
● No, don't go to any trouble. I'll just take some aspirin.
○ And try to relax a bit, O.K.?
● I know. I really have to calm down. I'm probably giving *you* a headache.
○ Hey, we all have our bad days.

Figure it out

Find another way to say it.

1. Someone should do something about that noise outside.
2. I'll have them turn it down.
3. I have a bad headache, and I can't stand that noise.
4. It could kill someone.
5. I hope they finish it all by tomorrow.

84

Ways to say it

Complain to your partner about a problem with noise. Your partner will suggest a solution.

- They're doing construction right outside my bedroom window, and the noise has been driving me crazy.
- ○ I know how you feel. I had that problem at work once.
- I just wish something could be done about it, though. It wakes me up at seven every Saturday.
- ○ Well, what if you slept with earplugs?
- Now that's a thought.

Some sources of noise	Some comments on a proposal
construction airplanes traffic dogs neighbors coworkers	Now that's a thought. It's worth a try. I guess it doesn't hurt to try. It's not worth the effort. It's more trouble than it's worth. It's too much of a headache.

2

THE PASSIVE WITH MODAL AUXILIARIES: PRESENT OR FUTURE TIME

Active

Someone	must	fix	the sidewalk.		an obligation
Someone	should	fix	the sidewalk.		a recommendation
The repairs	could would	prevent	an accident.		a result
That big hole	may might	injure	someone.	◀	a possibility
That big hole	must	annoy	people.		a logical conclusion
Someone	can	fix	the sidewalk.		ability
You	may can	file	a complaint.		permission
Someone	will	repair	the sidewalk.		future time

▲ base form

Passive

The sidewalk	must		fixed.
The sidewalk	should		fixed.
An accident	could would		prevented.
Someone	may might	be	injured.
People	must		annoyed.
The sidewalk	can		fixed.
A complaint	may can		filed.
The sidewalk	will		repaired.

▲ past participle

> Use *could* for a possible result and *would* for a more definite result. Compare:
>
> If they fixed the hole in the sidewalk . . .
> an accident *could* be prevented. (It's possible.)
> an accident *would* be prevented. (I'm sure of it.)

3 MAKE A COMPLAINT

Complain about a danger. Then say what you think should be done about it.

- Did you notice the hole in the sidewalk outside this building?
- ○ Yes. Someone could fall and break a leg.
- It really should be filled.

> You *fill* a hole, *fix* a pothole,
> *sweep up* glass, and *mop up* water.

Some dangers

a hole in the sidewalk
a pothole on a highway
broken glass on the floor
  of a store
water on the floor of a
  restaurant

sweep   swept   swept

4 MAKE A COMPLAINT

Write a letter to the traffic department, using at least three sentences with modal auxiliaries. Use the information in your notes.

Start like this:

Dear Sir/Madam:

I am writing to express my concern about a dangerous intersection at Warren Street and Porter Avenue....

Information to include:

Problem at Warren St. and Porter Ave.

- five accidents in three months--no traffic light or stop sign
- parked cars on both sides of the street--hard to see pedestrians
- school crossing (Porter Elementary School on Porter Ave.)--no crossing guard

Solutions

- install traffic light or stop signs
- prohibit parking on these streets
- assign a crossing guard to the intersection before and after school

5 OFFER TO DO SOMETHING

Make a complaint. Your partner will offer to do something to solve the problem.

- I'm starving, but I don't have time to go out for lunch.
- ○ I'll get | the restaurant to send up a sandwich | for you.
  | a sandwich sent up |
- Oh, you don't have to do that.
- ○ It's really no trouble at all.

Some situations

It's already two o'clock in the afternoon and you have too much work to do to go out for lunch.
You're in the hospital and you just noticed that your pitcher of water is empty.
You want to park your car, but a delivery truck is blocking your driveway.
It's very hot in the restaurant where you're having dinner, but the air conditioner isn't turned on.

THE CAUSATIVE *GET*

Active

| They're trying to | get | me you him her us them | to fix | the radiator. |
| | | | to stop | the noise. |

▲ infinitive

Compare:

They're trying to *have* him *fix* the radiator.
They're trying to *get* him *to fix* the radiator.

Passive

| They're trying to | get | the radiator | fixed. |
| | | the noise | stopped. |

▲ past participle

7 Alberto Lopez, who manages a drugstore, is talking to Sheila Evans, the assistant manager. Complete Sheila's part of the conversation, using the causative *get* or the causative *have* in either active or passive sentences.

Alberto: We're low on Band-Aids.
Sheila: Yes, I know. I'll talk to the supplier and _____ .
Alberto: Good, because the order may take up to a week to come in.
Sheila: Speaking of orders, they sent an order of shampoo to our other store by mistake. Do you want me to _____ ?
Alberto: Sure. Why should we have to pick it up? By the way, someone should unpack those two crates of deodorant in the back.

Sheila: O.K. I'll _____ .
Alberto: Jim won't be in today. Ask Harry. Hey, what's that puddle back there?
Sheila: Oh, someone broke a bottle of cough medicine. I'll _____ .
Alberto: One last thing. Bonnie forgot to fill out her timecard last week. Please talk to her about it.
Sheila: Don't worry. I'll _____ .

8 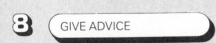 GIVE ADVICE

Your partner will complain about a headache. Give advice, referring to the article on pages 82–83.

● My head is killing me!
○ Maybe you're just hungry. What time did you eat lunch?
● I didn't. I was too busy to take a break.
○ Hunger is a common cause of headaches. I've read that eating something high in protein can help.

Some causes of headaches	Some situations
hunger eyestrain noise nervousness sun	You had a busy day at work or school and didn't eat lunch. You've been studying in the library all day. You and a friend are at a rock concert. You have the lead role in a play and are about to go on stage. You've been repairing telephone lines outdoors all day in the hot sun.

Your turn

1.

You have gotten together with a group of neighbors to complain about the "headaches" in these pictures. Work in groups to find solutions to each one.

2. Listen in 🔲

Read the question below. Then listen to the interview and choose *a*, *b*, *c*, or *d*.

How did Mr. Hatfield solve the problem of his neighbor's yard?
a. He got his neighbor to clean up the yard.
b. He got the yard cleaned up himself.
c. He called the police.
d. He wasn't able to solve the problem.

3.

Do you agree with the conclusion Mr. Hatfield reached? Discuss this question in groups.

4. On your own

Write a letter of complaint to your community newspaper, choosing one of the topics below.

1. Complain about one of the "headaches" in the pictures. Then offer a solution.
2. Complain about a real problem in your neighborhood. Try to suggest more than one solution for it if you can.

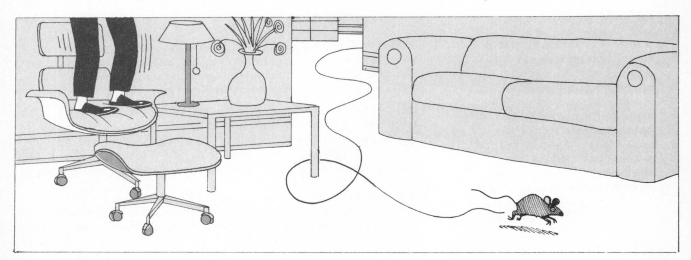

A YEAR LATER, LOTTERY PRIZE STILL A 'FANTASY'

by Suzanne Daley

Bernice and Louis Eisenberg at their new apartment.

BROOKLYN, N.Y., Nov. 15, 1982 — Although it has been a year, they still like telling the story — every wonderful detail — of when and how they found out they had won $5 million in the New York State Lottery.

Since then, they have traveled to Hawaii, California, and Las Vegas, Nevada. They have been to the ballet, tennis matches, and a dozen Broadway shows. They have talked with stars and been guests on television talk shows.

It was a year ago yesterday that Louis and Bernice Eisenberg became the first to win the lottery's top prize. All the bills are paid now. Mr. Eisenberg has retired from his job as a maintenance worker in a Manhattan office building. After twenty years of living in a small apartment with a close-up view of a red brick wall, the Eisenbergs have moved to an apartment with a seventeenth-floor view of the ocean.

"I always figured I'd have to work until I fell off the ladder," Mr. Eisenberg said. "It's a miracle. It's a fantasy."

Mrs. Eisenberg had cancer twelve years ago. She still worries about her health, and she often feels weak. "We've had a lot of problems. I figured God said, 'O.K. Bernice, you've had enough .'"

Mr. Eisenberg said that winning hadn't cost him any friends yet. "People have been really great. I think it's because it didn't happen to an executive.

"You have more toys to play with, but the values don't change," Mr. Eisenberg said. "My back still hurts. My neck is still stiff. That didn't change."

Over the last year, the Eisenbergs have collected a lot of funny stories. There's the one about how they went all the way to Hawaii — a lifelong dream — and got a hotel room that faced a parking lot. There's the one about the television interviewer who tried to call Mr. Eisenberg an electrician. "I had to tell him I was a light-bulb changer," he said.

The Eisenbergs have bought a video cassette player so they can watch the tapes of themselves on the television talk shows. "We play them sometimes if friends want to see them," Mr. Eisenberg said.

"Sometimes?" interrupted Mrs. Eisenberg. "Who is going to say no? I've heard them so many times, when he puts them on I go into the kitchen, and I can mouth every word."

The Eisenbergs would still like to do a lot more traveling. They also want to visit museums and read. The time just goes so fast, they said.

Figure it out

1. A lottery is a contest in which someone buys a ticket with a number or numbers on it in hopes of winning a lot of money. As you read the two articles, form your own opinion of lotteries. Then, based on what you have read, argue for or against this statement: "Buying lottery tickets is a waste of money."

2. As you read the two articles, look for ways that the experiences and opinions of the Eisenbergs are different from those of Ken Proxmire. Then decide who would make each comment below. Say *Louis or Bernice Eisenberg* or *Ken Proxmire*.

1. I wish I had time to travel more.
2. I tried to help my two brothers, but things didn't work out.
3. Your lifestyle changes a lot when you win a lot of money, and you have to be prepared.
4. Your lifestyle changes a little when you win a lot of money, but your values don't change.
5. I'd like to write a book about my experience.
6. I still have the same friends and the same health problems.
7. I lost a lot of money because I spent too much money too quickly.

Lottery Winnings Lead to Bankruptcy for Coast Man

FRESNO, Calif., May 8, 1982—Ken Proxmire thought the $1 million he won in the Michigan State Lottery was the answer to his dreams, but instead it has led to bankruptcy.

How does a man who is guaranteed $50,000 a year for the next 14 years end up bankrupt?

The 38-year-old businessman said it was easy. "Your lifestyle changes when you go from $15,000 to $50,000."

In Mr. Proxmire's case, the changes started immediately. He moved his family from the Detroit area to California and bought a new home, car, and clothes.

Mr. Proxmire wanted to buy a bowling alley, but he did not have the $500,000 he needed, and he could not get credit on his lottery winnings. So he bought a pool parlor.

Then he started to sell pool tables, too, opening stores in three cities in the San Joaquin Valley. He brought two of his brothers, along with their families, out from Michigan to act as his partners.

"But we expanded [our business] too fast," he said. "By the beginning of 1981, sales dropped because of high interest rates, so here I am stuck with three stores and three families to support."

Mr. Proxmire said he had already paid off nearly half of the $80,000 his business lost but could not pay off the rest.

And $50,000 a year does not seem like very much now, he said.

He said he had learned a lot from the experience and planned to write a book about it for future lottery winners.

---

3. Find the highlighted words and say what they refer to. The words are listed below in the order in which they appear.

1. enough
2. it
3. one
4. him
5. them
6. it
7. his
8. the rest
9. it

4. The suffix *-ful* changes nouns into adjectives, as in *wonderful* or *cheerful*. Using the information in the article, complete the paragraph with appropriate words from the list.

careful hopeful useful
cheerful painful wonderful

Winning the lottery was a _____ experience for the Eisenbergs but a very _____ one for Ken Proxmire. Mr. Proxmire wasn't as _____ as he could have been with his money. He plans to write a book, and he hopes other lottery winners will find it _____ .

A risky business

Julie Hart, a trainee, is talking with Sam Bradley, who has been a firefighter for ten years.

Try this

Discuss one of these topics with a partner:

1. If you won a million-dollar lottery, what would you do with the money?
2. Have you ever made a decision about money that you now regret? If so, what should you have done differently?

● Sam
○ Julie

● I'll be honest with you, Julie. Putting out fires is no job for a woman.
○ So they say. But I enjoy it. I feel as if I'm doing something really important for the people of this city.
● I heard you were in business school before this.
○ Yes, but I dropped out during the second year. If I'd finished, I would have made a lot of money eventually. I'm happier doing this, though.
● Julie, five years from now you'll be telling people, "I want to quit. I want to go back to something safer."
○ Hmm. Would you ever quit, Sam?

● Sure I would. In fact, pretty soon I'll be staying home all the time, just counting my money. I won't be risking my life fighting fires.
○ Oh, the lottery again. You're a dreamer, like everyone else here.
● No, I'm not. I don't waste my money on lottery tickets. I put my money into things I can see.
○ Do you mean you invest your money in things like art?
● No, no. I mean real estate. Just old buildings like the ones around here. I've bought one already and I plan to buy more. When I leave here, I'll really be making a lot of money.
○ Don't quit your job yet, Sam. Real estate is a risky business.

Figure it out

Say *Right, Wrong,* or *I don't know.*

1. Julie had been a business student.
2. None of Julie's friends think she should be a firefighter.
3. Julie plans to make a lot of money in business eventually.
4. Sam would like to quit his job.
5. Sam likes to play the lottery.
6. Julie will leave the fire department in five years.
7. Sam plans to make a good living in real estate.

Ways to say it

Play the role of each of these people. Your partner will try to imagine what you'll be doing in five years.

- ● My job is making me miserable. Selling sandwiches is no way to make a living.
- ○ I know what you mean.
- ● I wonder what I'll be doing five years from now.
- ○ Don't worry. With your business sense, you'll be managing a chain of restaurants by then.

> In the future continuous, *will ('ll)* or *won't* is followed by *be* and a present participle:
>
> You'*ll be managing* a restaurant.

---

2  FUTURE WITH *WILL* VS. FUTURE CONTINUOUS WITH *WILL*

Future

I	'll	return	the camera at 3:30.
We	won't	have	jobs this summer.

Future continuous

I	'll	be	taking	pictures until then.
We	won't		working	when we move.

Future

> Use the future with *will* to talk about a specific event in the future:
> I'*ll take* your picture at 2:00.
> In twenty years, I'*ll buy* a house by the seashore.

> Use the future with *will* with verbs such as *be, have, want,* and *like* to describe a future state:
> In twenty years, I'*ll have* a lot of money.

> Use the future with *will* to talk about an event that will begin at the same time as another event:
> I'*ll make* dinner when you get home. (I'll start dinner then.)

Future continuous

> Use the future continuous with *will* to talk about an ongoing activity in the future:
> I'*ll be taking* pictures all day.
> In twenty years, I'*ll be living* in a house by the seashore.

> Use the future continuous with *will* to talk about an activity that will already be in progress when another event takes place:
> I'*ll be making* dinner when you get home. (I'll start dinner before then.)

TALK ABOUT THE FUTURE

Complete the following conversations with future or future continuous forms of the verbs in parentheses.

1. ● The show _____ over at ten o'clock. (be) Can you pick me up?
   ○ Sure. I _____ in the parking lot when you come out of the theater. (wait)

2. ● I've never met Mr. Nelson, so how _____ I _____ him at the train station? (recognize)
   ○ Don't worry. He's a very tall, thin man, and he _____ a red jacket. (wear)

3. ● One day we _____ lucky and we _____ the lottery. (be, win)
   ○ You really think so?
   ● Oh, sure. In twenty years, we _____ anymore. (work)   We _____ it easy. (take)

4. ● What do you think you _____ a year from now? (do)
   ○ Good question. I _____ you know in a year. (let)

 IMAGINE THE FUTURE

Imagine what life will be like in a hundred years. Discuss your fantasies with a partner.

● It's amazing how fast things change. I remember when I'd never even heard of computers.
○ You know, I wonder what life will be like a hundred years from now.
● Well, maybe we'll be living on the moon....
○ I can just see it now. People will have their own rocket ships, and there will be traffic jams in outer space.

Do you envision...?
personal rocket ships
tiny, super-fast computers
one world language
trips to other planets
glass-covered cities

 DISCUSS POSSIBILITIES

Give your true opinion.

● Would you ever play the lottery?
○ If I had extra money, I would. Who knows? Maybe I'd be lucky.... Why? Would you?
● Me? Never. I think it's a waste of money.

Would you ever...?
play the lottery
live in a very cold climate
have more than five children
take a flight to the moon
shake hands with a space creature

6 **EXPRESS REGRET**

Complete the sentences. Then discuss one of your regrets with a partner.

● You know, sometimes I'm sorry I went into business.
○ Really? Don't you like what you're doing?
● Well, my job pays well, but it doesn't really interest me. If I'd gone to journalism school, I could have been a TV reporter.
○ There's a lot of pressure in journalism, though....

1. Sometimes I'm sorry I _____ .
2. If I'd _____ , I would have been happier.
3. If I'd thought about it more, I wouldn't have _____ .
4. If I hadn't _____ , I wouldn't have _____ .
5. If I'd _____ , I could have _____ .

CONTRARY-TO-FACT CONDITIONAL SENTENCES

Present time

	Past tense form	Conditional		
If	I had more money (I don't),	I would (I'd)	buy	a house.
	I were smart (I'm not),	I wouldn't	play	the lottery.
	he tried (he doesn't),	he could	find	a job.
	she weren't patient (she is),	she couldn't	be	a teacher.

▲ (base form)

Past time

	Past perfect form	Past conditional		
If	I'd had more money (I didn't),	I would have	bought	a house.
	I'd been smart (I wasn't),	I wouldn't have	played	the lottery.
	he'd tried (he didnt'),	he could have	found	a job.
	she hadn't been patient (she was),	she couldn't have	been	a teacher.

▲ (past participle)

8 **Read about the following situations. Then make a comment about each one with a present or past contrary-to-fact conditional sentence.**

1. The movie critics didn't like *Star Battles*, but Cara didn't read the reviews. She went to see the movie with a friend, and neither of them enjoyed it.
2. Carlos wants to retire, but he can't afford to. He would like to write his autobiography, but since he's still working, he doesn't have time.
3. Sarah always wanted to study architecture. Her parents told her it was a man's profession, so she became a teacher instead.
4. Toshio missed his plane because he got a flat tire on his way to the airport. He didn't have a spare tire in his trunk.
5. Denise went away on vacation without checking to see when her library books were due. When she returned them, she had to pay a large fine.

Your turn

1.

You are faced with a difficult choice. You can either continue to live in the present, or you can choose to live in a "futuristic" community of the year 2100. This community has the features shown in these photos from science fiction movies. Study the photos carefully and read the information in the box. Then, working in groups, discuss what life will be like in the new community. What will your decision be? Here are some questions to consider:

1. Will changes in technology improve the quality of life?
2. How will people's values and ideas be different?
3. What new problems will people face? What will cause these problems?
4. Why will the futuristic community be a better or worse place in which to live?

This Island Earth

This Island Earth shows how it will be important to communicate with visitors from other planets.

The city of the future in *Logan's Run* is covered by a glass dome. Buildings are shaped like pyramids and made of metal and glass.

In the future, according to *Things to Come*, we will have giant telescopes with huge screens. These will make it easy to draw maps for trips to other solar systems.

When Worlds Collide shows the importance of travel to other planets in rocket ships.

Forbidden Planet shows how robots may be used in the future. Here we see a scientist with Robby the Robot. Robby cleans the house, makes dinner, and washes dishes.

Logan's Run

Things to Come

When Worlds Collide ▶

Forbidden Planet

2. Listen in 🔲

Read the statements below. Then listen to a lecture by a futurologist, an expert on life in the future, and choose *a* or *b*.

1. The domes in the New Cities will _____ .
   a. protect people
   b. make it easier for people to travel
2. The weather in the New Cities will _____ .
   a. contain deadly meteor showers
   b. never be too wet or too cold
3. The workday in the New Cities will be short because _____ .
   a. the sun will shine only a few hours a day
   b. computers will save a lot of time
4. The Earth will be important to New Cities inhabitants because _____ .
   a. they will return to live there soon
   b. they will be interested in the past

3. On your own

Write a short essay, choosing one of the topics below.

1. You have just seen one of the movies in the photos. Using your imagination, think of a plot and write a movie review that describes the film's predictions for life in the future. Make sure to include your opinion of the movie.
2. You're a futurologist and have been asked to write a column for the magazine *New Directions*. Describe what you think life will be like in the year 2100.

What Is This Thing Called Love?

What is love? Dr. Michael R. Liebowitz, assistant professor of clinical psychiatry at Columbia University, believes that falling in love is influenced by our brain chemistry. This connection between the way we feel and the way our bodies function is the focus of Dr. Liebowitz's book,The Chemistry of Love. In an interview with People *magazine, he discussed his neurochemical theories of romance.*

Don't you find it upsetting to reduce an emotion like love to a chemical equation?

I'm a big believer in romance. The emotions we feel when we're in love are so powerful that when they're going on, nobody's going to stop to think about chemicals in the brain. Look at it this way. I know how digestion works. I know what goes on in my body when I eat something. But that has nothing to do with my enjoyment of a good meal.

What is love, chemically speaking?

I try to distinguish between romantic attraction and romantic attachment because I think they're chemically distinct. The symptoms of attraction — falling in love — are very much like what happens when you take an artificial stimulant. Your heart beats faster, your energy goes up, you feel optimistic. There are certain chemicals in the brain — phenylethylamine (PEA) is one — that produce the same effect when released.

What, then, is the basis for romantic attachment? What keeps us together?

There is an area in the lower brain called the *locus ceruleus* where feelings of panic and separation anxiety seem to begin. There are certain brain chemicals, called endorphins, that slow down the activity of the *locus ceruleus*. I believe that we're programmed at birth to produce endorphins when we're in close relation-ships. It's nature's way of keeping us together. When the relationship ends or when we're afraid that it might end, production of endorphins stops and we're thrown into a panic.

Why do people grow tired of each other?

What's intense in a relationship is the newness. That's why the great romances of literature are never between people who stay together. Romeo and Juliet, for example, never had a chance to get used to each other.

Why does being in love make everything in life seem wonderful?

Our pleasure centers need a minimum level of stimulation to function. Love lowers this level. When we're in love, it takes less stimulation to give us pleasure. That's why everything feels possible when you're in love, why everything looks rosy.

Do people work better when they're in love, or are they too distracted?

When people's emotional needs are being met, they work better. Love gives you more energy, more enthusiasm.

How do you keep love alive? How do you keep the PEA flowing in your own ten-and-a-half-year marriage?

You need newness, sharing, and growth. My wife changed careers lately. We shared that. She gave me a lot of ideas for this book. We were able to share that. We're buying a new home, an old farmhouse with some land. We'll be farmers together in a small way. All these shared changes are important. The brain has to experience a change, or there will be no excitement.

Figure it out

1. **After you read the first paragraph, say what you think the article is about. When you have finished the article, correct your answer if necessary.**

2. **As you read the article, pay attention to the statements Dr. Leibowitz makes to define and describe love. When you have finished, decide which of these statements are correct according to him. Say *Right* or *Wrong*.**

1. Romantic attachment is what people feel when they first fall in love.
2. Because of chemicals in the brain, falling in love can feel like taking an artificial stimulant.
3. Endorphins help to prevent separation anxiety.

4. People grow tired of each other when there is no newness to produce a chemical change in the brain.
5. When people are in love, they have trouble concentrating at work.

3. **Say *Same* or *Different*.**

1. pleasure
   enjoyment
2. optimistic
   depressed

3. attraction
   attachment
4. anxiety
   excitement

5. powerful
   very strong
6. effect
   result

4. **The suffix *-ment* changes a verb into a noun as in *enjoy* and *enjoyment*. First form nouns from the verbs in parentheses and fill in the blanks. Then complete each sentence appropriately.**

1. The _____ in a relationship goes away if... (excite)
2. When children grow up, their _____ to their parents... (attach)
3. I had trouble hiding my _____ when... (disappoint)
4. The most boring _____ I ever had in school was... (assign)

5. A boss should give employees _____ when... (encourage)
6. ..., but I haven't noticed any _____ . (improve)
7. ...gives me a lot of _____ (enjoy).

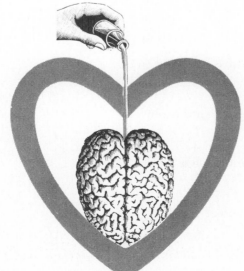

What a disaster!

Imagine that you're at a fancy restaurant with someone you want to impress. You're very nervous, and you spill your soup on the table. The soup then drips into the other person's lap. Act out a conversation for this situation with a partner.

Melinda is telling her best friend, Miki, about her first date with Ray. 📼

● Miki
○ Melinda

● So what happened on your date with Ray? Tell me all about it!

○ What a disaster! I was so embarrassed because of the way I looked. I had mud all over my dress.

● How did *that* happen?

○ Remember how it was pouring last night? Well, instead of watching where I was going, I was busy daydreaming. I tripped on a crack in the sidewalk, and the next thing I knew, I was sitting right in a puddle of water.

● (*Laughs*) I'm sorry. I didn't mean to laugh.

○ It may sound funny now, but it sure wasn't then. Poor Ray! He probably didn't know whether to laugh or cry.

● Oh, Melinda, don't take it so hard. Just think, you and Ray will never forget your first date!

○ If I ever hear from him again, that is.

● Oh, I'm sure you will. Anyway, you haven't even told me what you did last night.

○ Actually, we *did* see a pretty good movie. I guess you're right. It wasn't *all* bad....

Figure it out

Choose *a* or *b*.

1. Melinda was embarrassed _____ her dress had mud on it.
   a. because
   b. because of

2. Melinda was daydreaming instead of _____ attention.
   a. paying
   b. to pay

3. Melinda fell down _____ a crack in the sidewalk.
   a. instead of
   b. because of

4. Ray probably didn't know _____ to laugh or cry.
   a. if
   b. whether

Ways to say it

1 DESCRIBE AN EMBARRASSING EXPERIENCE

Think of an embarrassing experience you once had that seems humorous now. Share your experience with a partner.

● I'll never forget my first date. It was pouring out, and instead of watching where I was going, I was busy daydreaming. I tripped on a crack in the sidewalk, and the next thing I knew, I was sitting right in a puddle of water.
○ (*Laughs*) I'm sorry. I didn't mean to laugh.
● Oh, that's O.K. (*Laughs also*) It seems funny now, but at the time, I just wanted to crawl into a hole and die.
○ I can imagine!

Some expressions
I was so embarrassed.
I felt my face getting red.
I just wanted to disappear.
I just wanted to crawl into a hole and die.

2 SUGGEST AN ALTERNATIVE

You've made plans to do something with another student. Complete the sentences. Then use them to suggest alternatives to your plans.

● Listen, I'm a little tired tonight. Instead of going dancing, why don't we go to the movies? There's a good movie playing at the Valencia Theater.
○ That sounds fine. What time does it start?
● At 6:30, so let's meet in front of the theater at 6:15.
○ Hmm ... I have a meeting until 6:00. In case I'm late, go ahead and buy the tickets. I should definitely be there no later than 6:25.

1. Instead of going _____ , why don't we _____ ?
2. Instead of Friday, what if _____ ?
3. In case of rain, would you want to _____ ?
4. Because of the crowds, maybe we should _____ .
5. In case I'm late, _____ .
6. Let's _____ because _____ .

You've made plans to ...
go dancing.
go out to dinner.
go to the beach.
go to a popular movie.

 **3** **Close-up**   *BECAUSE, BECAUSE OF, IN CASE, IN CASE OF, AND INSTEAD OF*

The picnic is canceled	because	it's raining.		sentence
	because of	the rain.		noun
Dial 911	in case	there's an emergency.	◀	sentence
	in case of	an emergency.		noun
Let's take the càr	instead of	going by bus.		gerund
		the bus.		noun

4 The Grants are going out for the evening and leaving their son, Henry, all alone for the first time. Complete the conversation, filling in the blanks with *because, because of, in case, in case of,* or *instead of.*

Mrs. Grant: Now remember, _____ an emergency, call Mrs. Rivera. Here's her number.

Henry: Oh, Mom, nothing's going to happen. Why don't you just relax _____ worrying about me all the time?

Mr. Grant: We're just being practical, Henry. Now we want you to go to bed by 9:00 _____ school tomorrow. When we come home you should be sleeping.

Mrs. Grant: And _____ it starts raining, make sure to close all the windows. Please don't forget _____ I don't want to find water on the floor when I come home.

Henry: O.K. I won't forget. But _____ all these instructions, why don't you tell me what you left for dinner?

---

5 (EXPRESS UNCERTAINTY)

Think of a humorous situation in which you were unsure of what to do. Complete the sentences, and then use some of them to tell another student about your experience.

● I remember one time I was in an important meeting at work. I took off my sweater, and to my absolute horror a sock fell out!

○ You're kidding! What did you do?

● Well, I didn't do anything. I couldn't decide whether or not to apologize. I mean, I wasn't sure if anyone had seen it. So I just picked up the sock as fast as I could and put it in my briefcase.

1. I couldn't decide whether (or not) to _____ .
2. I didn't know whether to _____ (or not).
3. I was wondering if I should _____ .
4. I had trouble making up my mind whether to _____ or _____ .
5. I wasn't sure if anyone _____ .

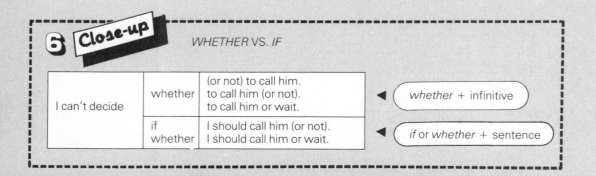

6 **Close-up**   *WHETHER VS. IF*

| I can't decide | whether | (or not) to call him.
to call him (or not).
to call him or wait. | ◄ *whether* + infinitive |
| | if
whether | I should call him (or not).
I should call him or wait. | ◄ *if* or *whether* + sentence |

7 TELL A JOKE

Complete the jokes, filling in the blanks with *whether (or not)* or *if*. In some sentences, both are correct.

1. "Now, sir," said the judge. "If you become a citizen, do you promise to come to the aid of your country whenever you are called?"

   "Well, Judge," the man replied. "I'm not sure _____ I can. My wife never lets me out of the house after work."

2. "Oh, so you're the chief of police of this nice little town," the woman said. "I'm so pleased to meet you. I wonder _____ I could shake hands with the fire chief, too."

   "Sure," the police chief answered. "Just wait until I change hats."

3. An angry man charged into a jewelry shop and shook his new watch in the owner's face. "You said this watch would last a lifetime," he yelled.

   The owner admitted, "I had trouble deciding _____ to tell you that. But you looked pretty sick the day you bought it."

4. "I can't decide _____ to have a slice of onion on my hamburger," the man said. "Do you think I'll get heartburn?"

   "Listen, mister," the waiter replied, "you get a hamburger for a dollar. Not medical advice."

8 TELL A STORY

Think of a childhood prank you played on someone or something naughty that you did. Write a paragraph, explaining how you tried to fool the person or how you misbehaved.

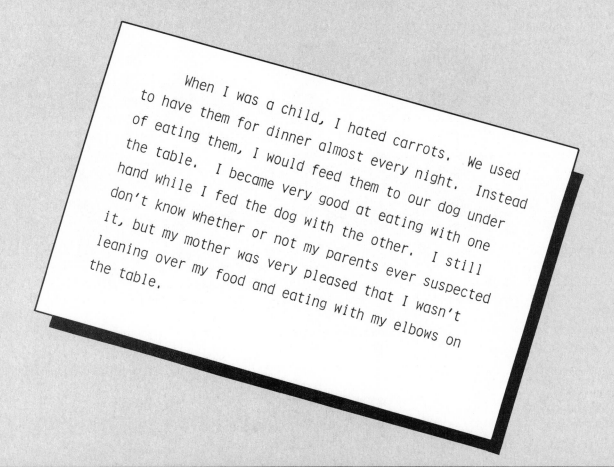

When I was a child, I hated carrots. We used to have them for dinner almost every night. Instead of eating them, I would feed them to our dog under the table. I became very good at eating with one hand while I fed the dog with the other. I still don't know whether or not my parents ever suspected it, but my mother was very pleased that I wasn't leaning over my food and eating with my elbows on the table.

Your turn

1.

One of the most popular forms of humor in many countries is the comic strip. Quino (Joaquin S. Lavado) was born in Mendoza, Argentina, and he created the cartoon strip *Mafalda* in 1962. Mafalda is the little girl in these cartoons, and the little boy, Guille, is her brother. Quino's cartoons have become world famous and have been translated into many languages. Work in groups to fill in the balloons, choosing the correct copy from the box below. Look at the artwork carefully, and discuss what details in the drawings add to the humor.

Mommy, was he your first boyfriend, or was someone else?

Good afternoon, what would you like?

And who are *you* thinking about, may I ask?!!!

All right! If you don't have soup, you don't get dessert!!

Will *everything* fit in here that they're going to teach me in school?

Good afternoon, what would you like?

But I only wanted to know if you were Mommy's first boyfriend . . .

How do you do. I just got here with my family, looking for some peace and quiet.

Listen, that's enough! Did you hear me? ENOUGH!!

I won't have any! I won't! I would be a disgusting person if there were some bribe that could make me sacrifice my principles, give up my beliefs, and betray my convictions!!

Good afternoon, I would like to speak to a grown-up . . . .

How I hate myself sometimes!!

Just a minute.

Now isn't the time for questions! Get to bed!

Crêpe suzettes . . .

2. Listen in 📼

Now look carefully at two more cartoon strips, both of which have somewhat serious themes. Listen to the conversations, and then, in your own words, write what each speaker is saying in each of the balloons.

3.

What is the author's point of view in these two cartoon strips? Do you agree with his opinions? Discuss these questions in groups.

4. On your own

Write a composition, choosing one of the topics below.

1. Explain why you think Quino's cartoons have been so popular. What makes them appeal to people, and why are they humorous? Cite examples from the cartoons.

2. Discuss another humorist who has impressed you, and explain why you like this person's work. You may choose a cartoonist, a comedian, or an author. Cite specific examples of this person's humor.

Quake's Eyewitness

'There came this horrible roaring, and the earth just started cracking.'

CHALLIS, Idaho, Oct. 28, 1983—Lawana Knox saw it happen.

"There came a horrible roaring," she said. Then the earth opened up before her eyes into an enormous crack 200 feet wide with terraced sides, like a staircase.

Her account of the Challis earthquake will be extremely valuable to scientists, said Dr. Spencer Wood, research professor of geology at Boise State University.

"She is only the first or second human being in modern history to observe a fault like this actually forming," he said.

Mrs. Knox fell to the ground and watched, horrified, as the earth split apart 150 to 200 yards in front of her. The massive crack spread for 15 miles along the base of the Lost River Mountains.

The earthquake, at 8:06 A.M., was measured at 7.2 and 6.9 on the Richter scale. It killed two children in this small town, injured three other people, and caused damage estimated between $2.5 million and $5 million. It also gave scientists a rare opportunity to look into the crust of the Earth.

Mrs. Knox and her husband, Bill, were hunting on a mountainside about 28 miles from their home when the earthquake occurred.

"At first, I heard a funny roar," she recalled. "I thought it was the wind blowing up the canyon—like it does, you know—except it was really still." When she saw the grass start to shake, she realized in the back of her mind that it was an earthquake, but she was more interested in hunting. "We've had tremors before," she said.

"The next thing I knew, [the force of the earthquake] had thrown the gun . . . out of my hands, and I couldn't get it. It felt as if somebody was shaking me by the shoulders, and I had the sensation that it would throw me on my face. I was disoriented. I sat down. . . . There was nowhere for me to go, so I just sat there and waited.

"Then there came this horrible roaring. I looked and the earth just started to open up . . . just dropping as if someone had taken a pair of scissors and started cutting."

Her husband was hunting at the top of a hill and did not see the fault line open up below, but he kneeled so he would not fall.

"I had the sensation that the world was rocking," he said. Mr. Knox decided to stay where he was until things quieted down.

Neither of the Knoxes was injured.

Dr. Wood brought 30 of his students from Boise to camp on the edge of the fault and study its size, shape, and formation. He told reporters that at no other time in history had there been an eyewitness to such an event whose account could be recorded and analyzed by geologists. The account would help to clarify exactly what had happened.

"It's magnificent," Dr. Wood said of the fault, "the largest to form in the United States since the 1950's."

Figure it out

1. As you read the article, look for answers to the questions below. When you have finished, adjust your answers if necessary.

1. What does the title refer to? What clues in the article help you understand the title?

2. Why are scientists interested in Lawana Knox?

2. Put these sentences in the correct order. Then use them and any other information you need to summarize the story briefly in your own words. Connect your sentences with expressions such as *All of a sudden...*, *Just then...*, and *Finally....*

___ Dr. Wood and his students came to study the fault.
___ The noise quieted down.
___ Mr. and Mrs. Knox went hunting.
___ There was a horrible roaring, and the earth split open.
___ Mrs. Knox heard a funny sound.
___ Mr. Knox joined Mrs. Knox at the bottom of the hill.
___ The grass started to shake.

3. Match.

1. crack (v)   a. feeling
2. human being   b. split apart
3. opportunity   c. person
4. occur   d. watch (v)
5. massive   e. chance
6. still (adj.)   f. unusual
7. sensation   g. happen
8. observe   h. enormous
9. rare   i. quiet

4. The suffix *-fy* changes an adjective into a verb meaning "to cause or make," as in *horrify*, "to cause horror." Very often, the suffix is added to a stem (*horr-*) rather than the complete noun (*horror*). Complete the sentences below with the correct form of a verb from the list.

beautify   fortify (to make strong)   identify
clarify   horrify   justify

1. The neighbors tried to _____ the neighborhood by planting flowers and trees.
2. After the earthquake, construction workers _____ all buildings in the area.
3. I think you should _____ the instructions before you give students this test.
4. It _____ Mrs. Knox to see the earth split open before her.
5. Three people were injured by the earthquake, but they have not been _____ .

The worst earthquake in the history of the United States took place in San Francisco in 1906.

107

Did you hear about the blackout?

Try this

Discuss one of these topics with a partner.

1. Have you ever joined a crowd that has gathered because of an accident, a fire, or a crime? What questions did you ask, and what did you find out?
2. Have you ever known anyone who has experienced a hurricane, an earthquake, or another type of natural disaster? What did the person tell you about his or her experience?

| ● Celia |
| ○ Phyllis |

Celia is talking to her friend Phyllis during a coffee break at work. 🔲

● Did you hear about the blackout downtown last night, Phyllis?
○ Yes, someone told me you were stuck in it.
● Not me—Paulo. He was in the theater office when all the lights suddenly went out. It was so dark that he had to use a flashlight to find his way.
○ People must have gone crazy. Did everyone panic?
● Fortunately, no. Paulo said people were mad because the movie had stopped, though. They kept asking if they were going to get their money back.
○ No kidding! What did he do?
● About the money? He promised them refunds.

○ No, I mean in general.
● Oh, well, he explained what had happened and told everyone to please stay seated.
○ That was smart. Someone could have been trampled, otherwise.
● Oh, Paulo was very careful. He had the ushers lead the people out one by one.
○ It all sounds pretty unpleasant to me. You know, I heard on the radio that the power didn't come back on until this morning.
● Did they say what had caused the blackout?
○ No, but it must have been caused by the heat. I'll bet every air conditioner in town was on last night.

Figure it out

Say *Same* or *Different*.

1. He told people to stay seated.
   He told people not to get up.

2. They kept asking him why the movie had stopped.
   Somebody asked him why the movie had stopped.

3. It must have been caused by the heat.
   The heat must have caused it.

4. I heard that the power didn't come back on until this morning.
   I heard that the power hadn't come back on yet this morning.

5. Someone could have been injured, otherwise.
   Someone was probably injured.

Ways to say it

REPORT AN EVENT

Read the newspaper articles. Then tell another student about the events.

● Hey, did you hear about the blackout last night?
○ No, I didn't. What happened?
● Well, it seems the entire downtown area was without lights. They interviewed the manager of a movie theater. He said it was so dark that he needed a flashlight to find his way.
○ I'm glad I didn't go to the movies last night. I would have been furious.
● People were. They kept asking if they were going to get their money back....

Why *has* the movie stopped? ▶ They asked why the movie *had stopped*.
Did people *panic*? ▶ A reporter asked if people *had panicked*.

When verbs that refer to states, such as *be* or *want*, are in the past tense in direct speech, use a past tense form in indirect speech:
Were people angry? ▶ He asked if people *were* angry.
Why *did* people *want* their money back? ▶ She asked why people *wanted* their money back.

Some expressions	
People	asked . . . kept asking . . . said . . . wondered . . . wanted to know . . .
The manager	told them . . . said . . . explained . . . assured them . . .

Clinton Neighborhood News

Heat Wave Is Probable Cause of Blackout

Investigators believe that this week's heat wave must have caused the massive blackout in the downtown area last night. Power was not restored in a three-mile area until 9:00 this morning.

"I was in the theater office," said Paulo Rodrigues, manager of Cinema 3. "All of a sudden the lights went out. It was so dark that I needed a flashlight to find my way."

"Luckily, no one panicked," Rodrigues told reporters, "but people were angry. They kept asking two questions over and over: 'Why has the movie stopped?' and 'Are we going to get our money back?'"

Citizen Cheered for Catching Purse Snatcher

Neil Franklin has become something of a local hero after recovering an elderly woman's purse from a thief on Market Street late yesterday afternoon.

"This is a very small town, and there's never been an incident like this around here," said eighty-year-old Beverly Walker, whose purse was snatched by a twenty-year-old man as she was crossing the street.

"My only thought was to help her," said Mr. Franklin, who was inside a store when he heard the woman cry for help. "So I went up to her and asked some questions: 'What does he look like?, What is he wearing?' — that sort of thing. She was very upset, but I told her, 'Stay calm. I'll get him.' And then I ran after him and caught him."

People cheered Franklin when he brought the thief to police headquarters.

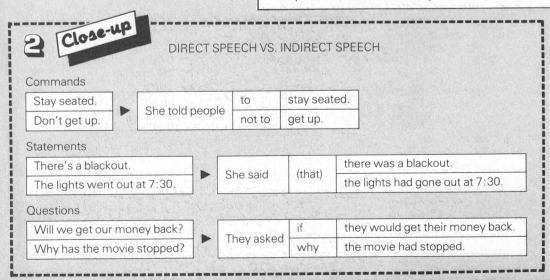

2 Close-up   DIRECT SPEECH VS. INDIRECT SPEECH

Commands

Stay seated.			to	stay seated.
Don't get up.	▶	She told people	not to	get up.

Statements

There's a blackout.				there was a blackout.
The lights went out at 7:30.	▶	She said	(that)	the lights had gone out at 7:30.

Questions

Will we get our money back?			if	they would get their money back.
Why has the movie stopped?	▶	They asked	why	the movie had stopped.

3 REPORT A CONVERSATION

During a recent air flight, you were seated next to a very nervous teenager. Report her conversation with a flight attendant, changing direct speech to indirect speech.

Captain:	The seat belt sign has been turned on. Please return to your seats.
Teenager:	Ooh! Is the plane going to crash?
Flight attendant:	Of course it isn't. This is simply a routine procedure. Everything is fine.
Teenager:	Then why did the captain tell us to fasten our seat belts?
Flight attendant:	Please don't worry. We've run into a little bad weather, but it won't be a problem.
Teenager:	Are you just trying to make me feel better?
Flight attendant:	No, really, there isn't any problem. Just try to relax.
Teenager:	Oh. Well, then, when can I take off my seat belt?
Flight attendant:	You can take it off as soon as the light overhead goes off.
Teenager:	Thank you. This isn't so bad after all.

Start like this:
There was a very nervous teenage girl next to me. It must have been her first flight. When the captain told us to return to our seats, she asked the flight attendant . . .

4 TALK ABOUT POSSIBILITIES

Read the newsbriefs. Then discuss the possible causes of these incidents with a partner.

- There was a traffic accident at the corner of Maple Street and Tenth Avenue yesterday. A truck hit a school bus.
- That's awful. Was anyone hurt?
- Fortunately, no, but someone could have been killed. The traffic light has been broken for a week.
- Is that what caused the accident?
- Well, it's hard to say. It might have been caused by drunken driving.

NEWSBRIEFS

MIDLAND, OKLA.—A truck carrying auto parts collided with a school bus at the corner of Maple Street and Tenth Avenue yesterday at 4:32 P.M. No one was injured, but both vehicles were seriously damaged.

Area residents reported that the traffic light at the corner had been broken since last Tuesday.

The truck driver was suspected of drunken driving, but he was not arrested.

NORTHFIELD, W. VA.—A West Virginia mine has been closed for inspection after an explosion yesterday morning trapped ten miners for over nine hours. A rescue squad was not called until two hours after the explosion because officials said they did not know that anyone was missing.

Miners at the Ridgewood Mine in Northfield had complained repeatedly about poor safety over the last several months. The mine has not been inspected regularly, and engineers are now looking into the possibility of a gas leak.

5 MAKE A JUDGMENT

Now make a judgment about each of the two incidents you discussed in exercise 4.

- ● It's a good thing no one was hurt in that accident at Maple and Tenth. The traffic light should have been repaired a lot sooner.
- ○ I agree. And if the driver was drunk, he should have been arrested.

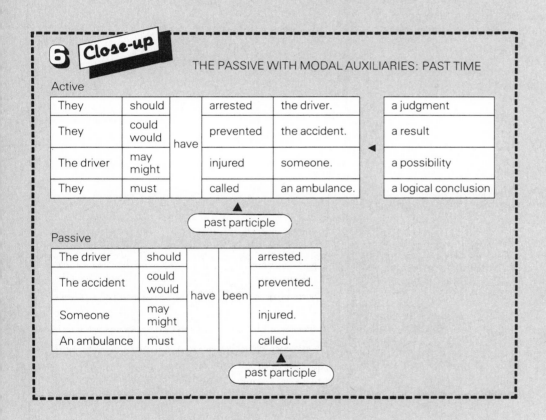

6 Close-up

THE PASSIVE WITH MODAL AUXILIARIES: PAST TIME

Active

They	should		arrested	the driver.	a judgment
They	could would	have	prevented	the accident.	a result
The driver	may might		injured	someone.	a possibility
They	must		called	an ambulance.	a logical conclusion

past participle

Passive

The driver	should			arrested.
The accident	could would	have	been	prevented.
Someone	may might			injured.
An ambulance	must			called.

past participle

7 Respond to each situation with a passive sentence about the past, using a modal auxiliary.

1. Countess Esterhazy left her famous diamond necklace in her hotel room and forgot to lock the door. When she returned, she discovered it wasn't there.

2. A two-thousand-pound statue in the plaza fell over yesterday. Fortunately, no one was hurt.

3. A fire started in an old wooden house on Main Street. The people who lived there tried to put it out by themselves. No one was injured, but most of the house was completely destroyed.

4. Jim Wells was having problems with his boss. They never seemed to agree on anything. One day Jim came out of his boss's office looking very unhappy.

Your turn

1.

Work in groups and study one set of illustrations carefully. Do not look at the other set. Then choose one of the three events and report on it to a group of students who has studied the other set of illustrations. You witnessed the event and you talked with many other people at the scene. Try to answer these questions:

1. What exactly happened? Did everyone who witnessed the event agree? Did the newspapers give the same description?
2. What do you think caused the incident?
3. How could the incident have been prevented?
4. Is there anything that should have been done that wasn't?

2. Listen in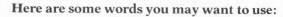

Read the paragraph below. Then listen to the conversation between two neighbors and complete the paragraph.

    Mrs. Harrison was upset because a(n) _____ had tried to _____ into her house. The _____ had escaped from the _____ but was finally _____ around 4:30. The _____ assured the Harrison family that the incident was very unusual.

3. On your own

Write a short news story, choosing one of the topics below.

1. Report on the event that your group described to another group of students.
2. Report on the event that another group of students described to you. Imagine that you interviewed these students at the scene of the event.
3. Report on an event that you have personally witnessed or an interesting event that you have read about in a newspaper.

Here are some words you may want to use:

Here are some words you may want to use:

elephant, escape (v), zoo, tent, statue, flood (n,v), laundry basket.

scatter, bucket, paint (n, v), spill, gun, mask.

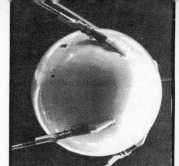

A copy of *Sputnik*.

Do space stations have a future?

The *Challenger*, the second space shuttle launched by the United States.

① Many years from now, when people regularly take their vacations in outer space, they will look back on the twentieth century and try to date the beginning of the space age. Some will say it all started with the launching of *Sputnik* in 1957, others will point to Neil Armstrong's first steps on the moon in 1969, and still others will mention the birth of the space shuttle — a spacecraft that could be used more than once to make space travel much less expensive. But at least a few will emphasize that the true beginning was the creation of populated space stations.

② A space station is actually a home in space. It is designed so many people can live and work there for a longer time than they would be able to in an ordinary, crowded spacecraft. The Soviet Union launched *Salyut*, an experimental station in 1971, and several teams of people were sent to the station to conduct experiments on how well people could live in space. In 1973, the United States orbited *Skylab*, its first experimental station, and in 1973 and 1974 three groups of astronauts conducted experiments there. Solar storms caused *Skylab* to fall from orbit in 1979, and it fell apart when it reentered the earth's atmosphere.

③ However, according to NASA,* the desire for a workable, long-term space station is still as strong as ever. In fact, the construction of just such a house is the next step in space science and exploration. Through the doors of a space station, spacecraft will leave for the moon or even Mars at a fraction of the cost of launching them from earth. In the space station's "rooms," astronauts and scientists will conduct important experiments in fields ranging from astronomy to chemistry, and industry will manufacture better products.

④ NASA's early plan for a space station called for 50 or even 100 people, including storekeepers, a barber, and a psychiatrist. While the space station that is now being planned is not as grandiose, it is still enormous and very complex. It will house half a dozen people. A central computer will control the climate in each section. Astronauts will dine on reasonably tasty, cooked food, and their average stay will be three to six months. There will be hot and cold water. The air will be a mixture of oxygen and nitrogen, just as on earth.

⑤ How will astronauts spend their days? NASA has a long list of possible activities. One laboratory will be devoted to animal and plant research and will be able to house as many as four monkeys and 200 rats. Another lab will be set up for laser, electronic, and similar high-technology experiments. Some companies already plan to manufacture rare drugs. Because there is no gravity, drugs can be produced that are purer; and they can be produced more efficiently.

⑥ If all goes well for the supporters of the space program, construction will begin in 1987 and be completed in 1992. The men and women who travel to outer space will then be able to make themselves at home in the sky.

⑦ And if space stations are successful, the next step may very well be space cities. One of the foremost space technologists involved in the planning of these cities is Gerard K. O'Neill of Princeton University. He expects the first space city to have a population of about 10,000. By the year 2050, there could be space communities of 100,000 to 10 million people.

⑧ Scientists believe that the benefits of space cities will far outweigh their costs. These space cities will help solve today's most pressing problems, among them overpopulation, the energy crisis, and pollution.

⑨ Yet, not everyone agrees that we even need a space station, let alone a space city. Many scientists think of what the money could buy here on Earth. "There's plenty of study and experimentation to do before we need [the space station]," says Victor Reis, former assistant director of the [Washington, D.C.] White House Office of Science and Technology. "What corporation would spend billions to construct a plant before either the manufacturing technology or the market were even established?"

⑩ But Gerald Griffin, director of the Johnson Space Center, thinks differently. "My suspicion is that the space station is like the telephone," he said. "No one thought they would need it when it was first invented, but once it was developed, everyone found they couldn't get by without it."

*[the United States] National Aeronautic and Space Administration

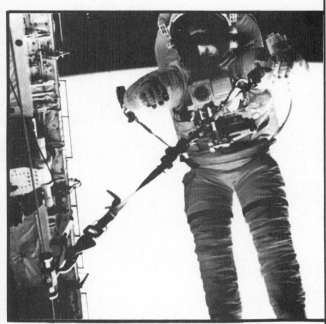

An astronaut testing safety techniques during a space walk.

A special sleep station on the *Challenger*.

Figure it out

1. **As you read, form an opinion on whether the article argues more strongly for or against spending money on space stations. When you have finished, give reasons to support your answer.**
2. **As you read, look for advantages and disadvantages of spending money on space stations. When you have finished, say *Right*, *Wrong*, or *I don't know* for each of the statements below.**

1. NASA is strongly in favor of building a space station.
2. It will be much more expensive to launch a spacecraft from a space station than from earth.
3. Space stations can be used to manufacture drugs more efficiently.
4. According to Victor Reis, we still don't have enough knowledge to make a decision on space stations.
5. Industries will make more money if they do their manufacturing in space.

3. **Find the paragraph that ...**

1. compares the space station to the telephone.
2. gives the history of the first space stations.
3. describes how complex NASA's future space station will be.
4. discusses plans for space cities.
5. gives reasons for opposing space stations.
6. describes the uses of space stations. (two paragraphs)
7. describes the benefits of space cities.

4. **Many words in English can be used as either nouns or verbs with no change in spelling or form. Find the words below in the article, and say if they are used as nouns or verbs. The words are listed in the order in which they appear.**

1. date	8. stay
2. work	9. list
3. house	10. house
4. step	11. plan
5. cost	12. travel
6. plan	13. study
7. house	

Compare:	
Noun	*Verb*
house	house
[háws]	[háwz]

115

I don't agree....

Which of the following do you feel a country should spend the most money on? Rank the items in order of importance from 1 to 6. Then discuss your decision with a partner, giving arguments to support it.

— child care — housing
— education — scientific research
— health care — space travel

A group of college students have gotten together for a discussion on the pros and cons of the space program. 🔲

Figure it out

Find another way to say the words or expressions in italics.

1. The space program is a waste of money. *What's more*, taxpayers are paying for it.
2. The space program has been expensive. *But* it has advanced science and created jobs.
3. *Even so*, the money should have been spent on cancer research.
4. People don't live in space now. *So* we should spend our money here on Earth.

● I think the space program is a waste of money. Think of all the research scientists could be doing on disease with that money.
○ Furthermore, the money is coming out of the taxpayer's pocket.
▲ I'll admit that a lot has been spent on the program. However, I don't agree that the money has been wasted. The research they've done for the space program has brought all sorts of advances in other areas —in geology, medicine, manufacturing ...
△ Not to mention all the new jobs the space program has created.
● Well, I suppose some people have benefited from the program. Nevertheless, I still wish all this money had been put into something more useful, like cancer research, for instance.
△ The space program *is* useful, though. Someday we may be able to use this knowledge to live in outer space.
○ Even if we understood perfectly how to live in outer space, the human race would never be able to survive there.
▲ How can you be so sure of that? Not too long ago no one would have believed we could go to the moon.
○ That may be, but the present is *here*, on Earth. Therefore, the money should be spent on the pressing problems the world faces right now.

Ways to say it

DEBATE AN ISSUE

Discuss one of these opinions in small groups, giving your true point of view. Use *what's more* or *besides* when you support an argument, *but* or *even so* when you counter an argument, and *so* when you draw a conclusion.

● I'm against teaching young children to cook. They usually make a mess and waste food.
○ I agree. Besides, children can hurt themselves.
▲ Even so, I think children *should* learn how to cook. Everyone should learn to be self-sufficient.
△ That's how I feel. Cooking isn't dangerous if children are taught safety rules.
■ Well, I'm in favor of teaching girls to cook, but it's a waste of time to teach boys.
□ I strongly disagree with that. Everyone eats, so everyone should know how to fix a meal.

Some opinions
Children should(n't) learn to cook.
Children should(n't) make their own decisions.
People should(n't) have to retire at a certain age.
Employees should(n't) call their bosses by their first names.
A person should(n't) get married before the age of thirty.

2 DEBATE AN ISSUE

Find a partner who agrees with you on one of these issues and, working in pairs, write a short editorial supporting your point of view. Then, if possible, exchange your editorial with a pair of students who took the other point of view, and write an answer to their editorial. Try to use some of the new expressions in the box.

Are you for or against . . . ?
banning smoking in elevators
having criminals do service in the community
spending more money on science
a twelve-month school year
more child-care programs for working mothers
socialized medicine

Some expressions	
First of all . . . Furthermore/Moreover . . .	◀ support an argument
However . . . Nevertheless . . .	◀ counter an argument
Therefore . . .	◀ draw a conclusion

Editorial

Ban Smoking In Elevators

As nonsmokers, we feel strongly that smoking in elevators should be banned. Elevators are small, enclosed areas, and breathing smoke is very annoying and unhealthy. Moreover, smoking in elevators is a fire hazard. Smokers seem to argue loudly about their rights. However, the rights of nonsmokers are rarely considered.

—Ramón Campos, Judith Sommers

Editorial Rebuttal

Smokers Have Rights, Too

We were disturbed by the anti-smoking editorial in last week's paper ("Ban Smoking in Elevators" 2/12/86). The authors claimed that smoke was annoying. This may be, but the attitude of these two authors is even more irritating. They say that everyone has rights. Therefore, the rights of smokers should be respected, too. One cannot deny that smoking is an unhealthy habit. Nevertheless, this is a personal concern rather than a public issue.

—Carol Marks, Roger Jenkins

3 **Close-up**

CONJUNCTIONS: *FURTHERMORE, MOREOVER, HOWEVER, NEVERTHELESS,* AND *THEREFORE*

Less formal

Smoking is unattractive.	What's more, Besides,	it is unhealthy.
Smoking is enjoyable,	but	it is bad for you.
Cigarettes are expensive.	Even so,	people keep buying them.
Smoking is a bad habit,	so	if you don't smoke, don't start.

More formal

Smoking is unattractive.	Furthermore, Moreover,	it is unhealthy.
Smoking is enjoyable.	However,	it is bad for you.
Cigarettes are expensive.	Nevertheless,	people keep buying them.
Smoking is a bad habit.	Therefore,	if you don't smoke, don't start.

In formal writing, do not start a new sentence with *but* or *so*.
If you are connecting two short ideas with the other conjunctions, you may use a semicolon (;) rather than starting a new sentence:

Smoking is unattractive; furthermore, it is unhealthy.

4 SUPPORT AN ARGUMENT

The principal of a high school recently gave a speech to the students. The speech would have been better if he had used more conjunctions. Rewrite the speech, using at least three of these conjunctions: *furthermore, moreover, however, nevertheless,* and *therefore*.

It has recently come to my attention that many students have not been attending classes regularly. This is a very serious situation. You cannot get good grades if you do not attend classes. You cannot qualify for a good job. It's true that many bosses don't look at grades. Bosses <u>do</u> want employees who are well educated, responsible, and have a positive attitude. I've heard several students say that classes are boring. If you have a positive attitude toward the material, you will see that it can be interesting. A good education is the most valuable of all possessions. I urge all of you to attend classes regularly.

EXPRESS REGRET

Discuss one of your regrets with another student. Use personal information.

● I wish I'd learned to play a musical instrument when I was young. I love classical music, and I've always wanted to play in an orchestra.

○ Well, it's not too late. I know you have a busy schedule, but maybe you should consider taking music lessons. What instrument would you learn to play? . . .

Do you wish you . . . ?
had learned to play a musical instrument
had majored in a different subject
had known your grandparents (better)
had stayed in touch with your old friends
hadn't moved when you were young
hadn't taken your present job

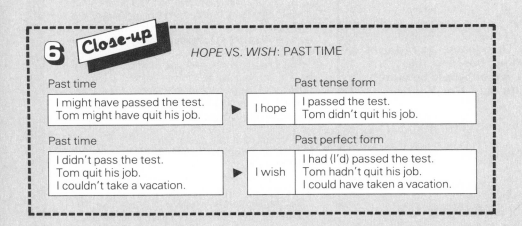

6 Close-up

HOPE VS. *WISH*: PAST TIME

Past time			Past tense form
I might have passed the test. Tom might have quit his job.	▶	I hope	I passed the test. Tom didn't quit his job.

Past time			Past perfect form
I didn't pass the test. Tom quit his job. I couldn't take a vacation.	▶	I wish	I had (I'd) passed the test. Tom hadn't quit his job. I could have taken a vacation.

 7

TALK ABOUT HOPES AND WISHES

Read about these people, and say what they hope and wish about the past.

1. Marie Laporte finally wrote to her friend Stella after three years. Two months later, she still hadn't gotten an answer, and now she's afraid Stella may have moved.
Marie hopes _____ .
She wishes _____ .

2. Eileen O'Brien wasn't paying attention, and she hit a big pothole. She is afraid she might have damaged her car.
Eileen wishes _____ .
She hopes _____ .

3. George Burke gave a speech yesterday. When he got home, he realized he'd left his briefcase in the auditorium.
George hopes _____ .
He wishes _____ .

4. Masa Asato wanted to keep working full-time, but his company asked him to retire. Masa had an interview to be a part-time consultant at another company.
Masa wishes _____ .
He hopes _____ .

Your turn

1.

Read the newspaper articles. The highlighted words are important for understanding the articles, so try to figure out from the context what they mean. As you read, form your own opinion on these issues: censorship of violence on TV, physical punishment of children in school, and government funding for the arts. Then, working in groups, argue for or against one or more of the issues. Try to support your argument with information in the articles or with your own examples.

2. Listen in 🔲

Read the statements below. Then listen to a radio discussion on another topic and, based on the opinions in it, decide which person would be more likely to make each statement. Say *Mrs. Young* or *Dr. Torres*.

1. Children who move all the time may have trouble in school.
2. People who move a lot are more tolerant and open-minded.
3. Children who move a lot find it easier to get used to new situations later in life.
4. Moving frequently can put a lot of stress on a couple's marriage.

3. On your own

Write an editorial for a newspaper, choosing one of the options below.

1. Give your opinion on one of the issues you discussed in groups or on the issue you listened to. Support your argument, counter any opposing arguments, and then draw a conclusion.
2. Support your point of view on any issue that is of concern to you. Draw a conclusion if possible.

Violence in Rock 'n' Roll Videos

Hillside, Nebraska, usually a quiet town, was the scene of controversy last weekend as a parent group tried to ban the sale of cassettes of rock videos that have violence in them. It has been estimated that there are 17.9 instances of violence for every hour of rock video.

Twenty parents carrying signs saying, "Stop Violence in Our Neighborhoods" and "Keep Your Children Out of Jail," demonstrated in front of several stores where cassettes of rock videos are sold.

The parent group said a video called "Rock School" by a group called Heaven was typical. Here, high-school punk rock stars throw their books in the trash, and they are chased by a school guard with a rifle and a Doberman pinscher. The principal is wearing a stocking mask. The video ends with students and teachers rioting to rock 'n' roll.

Michael Jackson's "Thriller," in which monsters rise out of their graves and chase and threaten a woman, was also criticized. "This man is a hero to our young people," one woman said of Jackson, "and he's encouraging violence against women."

Teenagers who were interviewed outside one store were outraged by the demonstration. "To assume that young people will do whatever they see or hear doesn't say much for their intelligence," said Shelly Woods, 17. "Our world is far from perfect, and teenagers must be taught at home to judge what is right and wrong," added Greg Bryant, 18. "Censorship is not the answer."

Family Sues School For Slapping Child

A Westway couple was awarded $15,000 by a circuit court judge after their ten-year-old son accidentally had a tooth knocked out when he was slapped by his teacher, Mrs. Gertrude Wells, 47.

In his testimony, Robert Farrington, 10, described how his teacher had slapped him across the face for bringing a live frog into the classroom and "creating a serious disruption."

Mrs. Wells may face suspension, depending on the decision of the local school board.

"I am extremely sorry about the tooth," commented Mrs. Wells, "and I did not mean to lose control. This child, however, was always misbehaving. I was really fed up with him. This was the third time in a week I had lost at least a half-hour of class time because of his behavior."

LOW-INCOME HOUSING FOR ARTISTS APPROVED

SAN FRANCISCO, Ca., May 30—The housing commission has approved the conversion of two apartment buildings on Sunrise Street to low-income housing for artists, writers, and people in the performing arts.

Although some local artists felt the decision was "long overdue," there was a great deal of opposition in the community. "These buildings provided low-income housing for poor families," said one area resident. "They will now be forced out into the street."

"I feel sorry for the families who will have to move," commented Sally Fisher, a dancer. "However, if the arts are going to survive, the government will have to support them."

Punk's Hair Apparent

by Eloise Salholz with Sonja Steptoe, and Elizabeth Bailey

It started on the streets of London nearly ten years ago with shaved heads, spiked haircuts, and Mohawks. Today, punk hair has arrived on the typical street in the United States. The wild look of the original has been changed for the larger market, but you can still see the shaved heads and off-center cuts.

For the last several years, women have been wearing their hair long, loose, and un-shaped. But no more, if stylists have their way. Hairdressers are creating a look that many call "postpunk." In the fall of 1984, leading hair stylist Christiaan introduced hair styles that were off-center, stiffened, sometimes close-shaved — and almost always short.

It didn't take long for the hair-care industry to be influenced by these new trends. Products that can be used to slick back hair or shape it into spikes are flooding the market. Christiaan has his own prescription for shaping hair more easily: don't use shampoo (he hasn't in seven years), just rinse it, "like salad." And the adventurous can color their hair with dyes that are easy to wash out. One hairdresser predicts that wild colors will appeal to more people and will be accepted faster than wild cuts. You can dye your hair green for a party and wash it out the next morning, but if you've shaved your head you're stuck with it.

For some kids, however, only true punk will do. For them, it's not only a matter of fashion, but of principle. "I know I'm not going to spike my hair forever," said one eighteen-year-old, "but even if I wear [clothes by the designer] Saint Laurent, I'll still have the same ideals."

The Face of Things to Come

If you're bored with your face, it may be time to try something new, like messy lipstick, striped cheeks, eyeshadow that doesn't match, or even some words painted on your face to tell everyone how you feel.

"Make-up is fun, so people should enjoy it more," says make-up artist Linda Mason. Mason has created a look that is sometimes called "post new wave." "It doesn't have to be perfect to be beautiful," Mason says.

Cosmetic companies expect face-painting to increase sales and make women more adventurous in their choice of colors. "The lesson to learn from Mason," says one beauty expert, "is that there are no more rules."

1 As you read the article, try to figure out what "Punk's Hair Apparent" refers to. When you have finished reading, decide which sentence below best expresses the meaning of the title. Choose *a* or *b*.

a. There are still many people who have the original punk hair styles.
b. The influence of the original punk hair styles can be seen in many new hair styles.

2 As you read the article, look for ways that "punk hair" has influenced more recent hair styles. When you have finished reading, skim the article again and say *Right* or *Wrong* for each statement below.

1. The punk look started in London, but now "postpunk" has become popular in the United States.
2. Long, loose hair used to be in fashion. However, it does not appeal to many hairdressers now.
3. Although leading hair stylist Christiaan was doing punk styles in the fall of 1984, he's only doing traditional styles now.
4. Christiaan's styles require clean, shiny hair. Therefore, he recommends a daily shampoo.
5. Not many people will use strange hair dyes because none of them wash out.
6. Linda Mason believes that make-up should be put on very carefully and should never be messy.

Review 16

3 This editorial by a student recently appeared in a high-school newspaper. Complete the editorial. Fill in the blanks, choosing from these conjunctions: *although, because, furthermore, however, nevertheless,* and *therefore.*

I am a senior who is very offended by the new regulation prohibiting "punk" haircuts. I do not have a punk haircut myself, and I do not even like the punk cut. _____, I believe schools should not tell students how to wear their hair.

Most teachers are not opposed to punk hair. _____, our principal admits that "a wild haircut does not necessarily mean wild behavior." This regulation is in effect only _____ a few parents have complained.

A small group of parents should not be allowed to determine school policy. _____, I hope our principal will reconsider this new regulation.

4 Magazine writer Maureen Williams is talking with clothes designer Marti Sandoval. Complete their conversation, filling in the blanks with future or future continuous forms of the verbs in parentheses.

Williams: What are your plans for next spring's collection?
Sandoval: To tell you the truth, I'm not answering any questions yet. (*Laughs*) You _____ your answer next month when my catalogue is ready. (get)
Williams: Well, I _____ for it! (wait)   Tell me, how do you get ideas for new styles?
Sandoval: Well, I just watch what people are wearing. For example, I _____ in France and Italy next month, and I _____ for new ideas the whole time. (be, look)   If I see anything exciting, I _____ a drawing of it right away. (make)   And I always plan well ahead of time. By the time you receive my spring catalogue, I _____ on designs for next winter. (work)
Williams: How about the future? How are styles going to change over the next twenty years?
Sandoval: I think styles _____ more conservative. (become)   A lot of people _____ their money on computers instead. (spend)

5 Sally is the adventurous type, but her friend Janet doesn't like anything new or different. Complete Janet's responses, using a sense verb and *like, as if,* or *as though* in your answers.

1. Sally: Cindy's punk haircut is certainly interesting.
   Janet: I don't think so. _____ .

2. Sally: Listen! They're playing the new Bruce Taylor album.
   Janet: You call that music? _____ .

3. Sally: Isn't that a terrific painting of a mother and child!
   Janet: Is that what it is? _____ .

4. Sally: Here, try this caviar omelet. It's delicious.
   Janet: Ugh! _____ .

5. Sally: Isn't the guest speaker interesting?
   Janet: I don't think so. _____ .

Special Ailments Can Silence the Music

by Barbara Zigli

Before you read the article, try to figure out what the title means. When you have finished reading, explain the title in your own words.

While athletes worry about tennis elbow and jogger's knee, musicians have their own set of problems: horn player's palsy, fiddler's neck, cymbal player's shoulder, and flutist's chin.

At best, those problems are a temporary annoyance that can lower the quality of a top performance. At worst, they ruin a musical career.

"There isn't a lot in the medical literature about these things," says Dr. Richard Lederman of the Cleveland Clinic. "The area is where sports medicine was 15–20 years ago — just beginning to draw some interest."

To encourage that interest, the Cleveland Clinic and Music Associates of Aspen (Colorado) are co-sponsoring a conference on "Medical Problems of Musicians," in Aspen.

"When we talk about musicians, we're talking about millions of people, from school kids to the adult amateur to the professional," says Dr. Howard L. Levine, a Cleveland Clinic specialist in nasal, sinus, and throat problems.

Most musicians report some physical problems, Lederman says, and most can be treated or cured with physical therapy, exercise, and medication.

Common ailments include:

- Tightness of the lips and facial muscles among horn players.
- Skin lesions on the necks of violin and viola players.
- Finger numbness or a facial rash from flute-playing.
- Pain and tightness in the upper arms of cymbal players.
- Enlargement of the throat or temporary paralysis of the soft palate of woodwind players.
- Hearing loss among musicians sitting near the percussion section.
- And the dreaded Diplacusis, a hearing disorder that causes a musician to hear two different tones when a single tone is played.

As you read, look for surprising facts about musicians. When you have finished, complete the statements below with *because, because of, in case, in case of,* or *instead of.* Then skim the article again and say *Right, Wrong,* or *I don't know* for each statement.

1. A musician's career may be ruined _____ health problems.
2. To prevent health ailments, young people should choose stringed instruments like the violin, _____ playing wind instruments like the flute or horn.
3. _____ a muscle injury, a musician should first consult a physical therapist.
4. A musician with Diplacusis hears two notes _____ one.
5. There isn't much to read on the health problems of musicians _____ doctors are just becoming interested in the subject.

3 Oliver Davis recently started taking violin lessons, and he's developed a painful blister on his finger. Restate the nurse's part of the conversation, changing the sentences in brackets to the passive. Omit the agent where it isn't necessary.

Nurse: [You should cover this blister] until it heals.
Oliver: So I can't take the bandage off at all?
Nurse: No, except that [you must change it once a day.] Also, [you should apply this cream] once a day.
Oliver: Can I practice the violin?
Nurse: No, because [it might irritate the blister.]
Oliver: But I'll forget how to play!
Nurse: Oh, [the cream will heal the blister] in less than a week.
Oliver: I hope I won't get another blister when I start to play again. Oh, by the way, I have an appointment next Thursday, but I'm going out of town that day.
Nurse: Just talk to the receptionist. I'm sure [she can change your appointment] to Wednesday.

4 Greg is a cymbal player whose arms are killing him, and he's having trouble doing his job at a grocery store. Give the manager's responses to Greg's statements, using the causative *get* or the causative *have* in either active or passive sentences.

Greg: These boxes are in the way, and I don't think I can move them.
Manager: _____ .
Greg: I'd really appreciate it. Uh, those bottles of juice that were just delivered—I don't think I can carry them, either.
Manager: Well, Steve's here today. _____ .
Greg: I'm afraid I'm going to have trouble putting those jars on the top shelves, too.
Manager: I'm sure Shelly wouldn't mind helping out. _____ .

Greg: Wasn't I supposed to put up new signs in the windows today?
Manager: Yes, but don't worry. _____ .
Greg: Oh, thank you. This has never happened to me before. I can't even drive my car!
Manager: You mean you walked here! _____ . If I can't find anyone, I'll drive you home myself.

5 Kenneth, a make-up artist, is talking to Ruth, a singer, before a rehearsal for a TV show. Read the questions below. Then listen to the conversation and answer them. 📼

1. What are Ruth's two health problems? Which one is worrying her and why?

2. If Kenneth had the same two health problems, which one would cause him a lot of trouble at work? Why?

125

Arctic Yields Victims from 1848

EDMONTON, Alberta, Sept. 25, 1984 — Anthropologists have found the perfectly preserved remains of two British sailors who were frozen for 136 years in the central Arctic. They had been members of an unsuccessful search for the Northwest Passage.

The graves of a 20-year-old petty officer and a 25-year-old able seaman were found last month by scientists who were digging in the frozen ground of Beechey Island. The sailors had been members of Sir John Franklin's search for a water route connecting the Atlantic and Pacific Oceans.

Owen Beattie, a University of Alberta anthropology professor and leader of the university expedition, said the sailors' remains looked "more alive than dead." A third grave has been located, he said, but the body has not been removed.

"It's very exciting because it's almost like a time machine," Beattie said. "In fact, it is a time machine seeing people who look as they did 136 years ago, wearing their clothing.

"The hands [of the petty officer] were most touching," Beattie said. "They were very delicate, like a piano player's, and they looked as if they were warm."

John Franklin began the search for the Northwest Passage with a crew of 138 in May 1845. His ships were crushed by ice and abandoned on April 22, 1848. All crew members died.

1 Before you read the article, try to figure out what the headline means. When you have finished reading, explain the headline in your own words.

2 Rewrite this summary of the story, putting the sentences in brackets into the passive and omitting the agent where it isn't necessary.

In May 1845, [Sir John Franklin began a search for the Northwest Passage.] [A crew of 138 British sailors accompanied him.] On April 22, 1848, [ice crushed his ships] in the central Arctic, and [it killed all crew members.] Now [anthropologists from the University of Alberta have found the graves of three of the seamen.] [Scientists found the first two graves] last month. They said that [the ice had perfectly preserved the remains of two sailors.] [They have located a third grave,] but [they have not opened it] yet.

3 Complete the paragraph from an encyclopedia, filling in the blanks with appropriate quantifiers, comparatives of quantifiers, or quantifiers with partitives. Use the information in the box. Some items have two answers.

Early Explorers of the Western Hemisphere 1497–1789	
Nationality	*Number of Explorers*
Spanish	19
English	7
French	5
Portuguese	4
Italian	4
Canadian	1

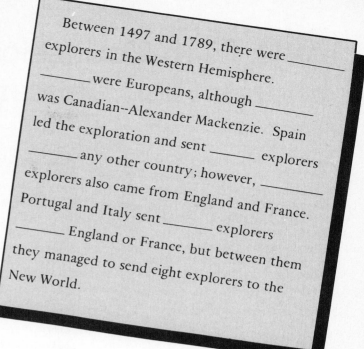

Between 1497 and 1789, there were _____ explorers in the Western Hemisphere. _____ were Europeans, although _____ was Canadian--Alexander Mackenzie. Spain led the exploration and sent _____ explorers _____ any other country; however, _____ explorers also came from England and France. Portugal and Italy sent _____ explorers _____ England or France, but between them they managed to send eight explorers to the New World.

4 Leon Baker is supposed to go camping in the mountains with you and some other friends. He's never been camping before. Report your conversation with him, changing direct speech to indirect speech.

Leon: I'm a little nervous about the trip.

You: Don't worry. Everything will work out fine.

Leon: Have you ever gone camping there before? How do you know it's safe?

You: My brother has been there twice, and I've seen all his photos. It's a beautiful place—safe and comfortable.

Leon: But . . . are there bears?

You: They won't come near us unless we leave food out. Please, stop worrying so much!

Leon: I'm sorry. I can't help it, but I'll try to relax.

> When a sentence has more than one verb, the form of each verb changes in indirect speech:
>
> I'*m* sure it'*s* safe. ▶ He said he *was* sure it *was* safe.

5 Paula and Roy Collins went fishing in Alaska in a rubber boat. The boat sank and now they are complaining to the manager of the store where they bought it. Restate the sentences in brackets by putting them in the passive and omitting the agent where it isn't necessary.

Roy: [Someone should have inspected that boat!] We're lucky to be alive.

Manager: Sir, [someone must have inspected the boat] at the factory.

Paula: Well, [they must not have done it] very carefully.

Manager: I'm not so sure about that. [A rock might have cut the underside of the boat,] or [the rough water may have caused the accident.]

Paula: [Then someone should have designed the boat] better. Boats are supposed to float, not sink!

Roy: [That accident could have killed us.]

Manager: Just let me write down your names. . . .

At 14, Teen Counselor Shares Their Concerns

by Lauren Long

If you're a teenager with a problem, fourteen-year-old Mark Godes can help. Since 1982, he's written a weekly advice column for teens under the name of Bobby Simpson. "I can relate to their problems," says Mark. "I'm going through them myself."

Here's his answer to a fifteen-year-old boy, whose mother felt he was too young to have a serious relationship with a girl who lived far away:

Your mother does have a point. Fifteen is a little young to be involved in a serious long-distance relationship. But I do think you should keep up your correspondence with your girlfriend. When you get older, and if you have still kept up correspondence with this girl, then you can go steady with her.

The column was Mark's idea. When he was eleven, he convinced a newspaper editor of his writing ability with seven sample columns he had created. Now he earns $50 for each column.

"I had read some letters written by teens to adult columnists, and I didn't think the answers were satisfactory. I try to write on the teenagers' level, but I don't talk down to them. It's just that their problems are closer to heart to me," he said.

Much of Mark's advice is clearly sensible. That's because, he explains, most of the answers are obvious.

"The big problem teens face is pressure from friends to smoke or drink. They don't want to be social outcasts and therefore are pressured into these bad habits. I can tell them not to get involved with certain people, and to . . . believe in their values.

"An adult columnist wouldn't understand. I've experienced peer pressure myself, but I've made the sacrifice of not being as popular as I could be," he says.

"I feel I have an insight into certain . . . problems," Mark added. "I've lived through a lot of problems myself. For two years since the column has been running, I've had to balance school, career, family, and friends. I've lost some of my social life because of work on the column. But I'm happy I've done it. Sometimes I'd rather be out playing basketball than writing a column, but it's great to know people are reading what you write and listening to you."

---

1. As you read the article, try to figure out Mark Godes's main reasons for writing a column for teenagers. When you have finished reading, answer these questions.

1. According to Mark, what is one big problem teenagers face? What did Mark do when he was faced with this problem himself?
2. Why does Mark feel he's a good columnist for teenagers?
3. If you were teenager with a problem and wanted advice, would you write to Mark or to an adult columnist? Why?

Dear Nancy,

[I'm not very happy, and the reason is my little sister.] For example, last night I was talking on the phone instead of doing my homework. My little sister was listening at the door. [I got in trouble only because she told my parents.] I think she actually wanted to see me get punished.

Last week I failed a math test, but I didn't show it to my parents. [Nobody knew about it until my little sister looked through my papers.] Of course she told my parents.

I don't think this is fair. [She keeps telling on me because my parents always take her side.] What should I do?

-- the brat's brother

---

2 Rewrite this teenager's letter to an advice columnist, changing the sentences in brackets to present or past contrary-to-fact conditional sentences.

Start like this:
Dear Nancy,
If I didn't have a little sister,
I would be a lot happier. . . .

3 Read about the problems of these teenagers. Then say what they hope and wish about the past.

1. Susie tried out for the gymnastics team, but she doesn't know if she was chosen. She's worried because she didn't exercise before the tryouts.
Susie hopes _____ .
She wishes _____ .

2. Maria's high school offers only one Italian class but two German classes. Maria wanted to take Italian, but there wasn't enough room in the class. She took German, even though she's not good at it, and now she's afraid she failed the test yesterday.
Maria hopes _____ .
She wishes _____ .

3. The Drama Club had auditions for a play yesterday. Peter was nervous when he tried out for a part.
Peter hopes _____ .
He wishes _____ .

4. Jason likes Polly, another thirteen-year-old. He's too shy to talk to her, so he wrote her a love letter and put it on her desk at school. Polly never said anything about the letter.
Jason hopes _____ .
He wishes _____ .

4 Complete the conversation between two teenagers, filling in the blanks with *whether* or *if.*

Andrea: What are you going to do this summer?

Terry: I haven't decided _____ to work at the grocery store or take care of people's yards. How about you?

Andrea: To tell you the truth, I don't know _____ I should work at all this summer. I've had so much trouble with math this year. I'm still trying to decide _____ or not to go to summer school.

Terry: Well, it's up to you. Personally, I'm not sure _____ I could stand going to school in the summer.

5 Read the advice column. Then rewrite the article, changing the sentences in brackets to the passive and omitting the agent where it isn't necessary.

Dear Dr. Lee:

I've looked everywhere for an after-school job with no luck. Any suggestions?

— Frustrated

Dear Frustrated:

Many teenagers have written to me on this topic. Perhaps you will get some ideas from Carol Janus, who was interviewed by the Bedford Democrat. I've reprinted the article, with permission of that paper.

An Enterprising Youth

Meet Carol Janus. She is only thirteen years old, but [she has already planned her future.] She wants to be a veterinarian, own her own home, and have at least two horses. [Someone will have to pay her college tuition,] and Carol has already begun to save.

[Companies can't hire boys and girls who are under sixteen years of age,] so Carol looked for work around the neighborhood. She knew that [nobody needed one more baby-sitter,] and she discovered that [kids had taken all the paper routes.]

As a result, Carol decided to start her own service as a plant- and pet-sitter. Now when people go on trips, they call Carol. ["No one has done anything like this] around here before," said one happy client. "Many plants might have died and [people would have put the pets] in a kennel. Now [someone waters the plants,] and [someone takes care of the pets] at home."

Carol Janus is not just a dreamer. She is doing something _____ come true.

129

Grammar appendix

Verb tenses

PRESENT TENSE OF *BE*

	Are	you they	from	Rio?
Where	is	he she	from?	

I	am ('m) 'm not		
We They	are ('re) aren't ('re not)	from	Brazil.
He She	is ('s) isn't ('s not)		

SIMPLE PRESENT

	Do	you they	work	near here?
Where	does	he she	work?	

I We They	work	in a hospital.
	own	a grocery store.
	teach	at Brooklyn College.
He She	works [s]	in a hospital.
	owns [z]	a grocery store.
	teaches [əz]	at Brooklyn College.

have	do	go
has	does	goes

I We They	don't	work	near here.
He She	doesn't		

PRESENT CONTINUOUS

	Are	you they	watching	TV?
What	is	he she	doing?	

I	am ('m) 'm not		
We They	are ('re) aren't ('re not)	watching	the movie.
He She	is ('s) isn't ('s not)		

PAST TENSE OF BE

	Were	you they	at work on Friday?
Where	was	he? she?	

I He She	was wasn't	at home. at work.
We They	were weren't	

SIMPLE PAST

	Did	you he she they	like have	the movie? a good time?

I He She We They	liked [t]	it a lot.
	enjoyed [d]	the party.
	wanted [əd]	a new car.

I He She We They	didn't	like	it at all.
		enjoy	the party.
		want	a big car.

What	did	they	want?

PAST CONTINUOUS

	Were	you they	eating	dinner?
What	was	he she	doing?	

I He She	was wasn't	eating	dinner.
We They	were weren't		

FUTURE WITH *WILL*

	Will	you they	get	here soon?
When	will	he she	get	here?

I He She We They	will ('ll) won't	arrive	soon.

PRESENT CONTINUOUS AS FUTURE, FUTURE WITH *GOING TO*, AND FUTURE WITH *WILL*

What are we	having	for dinner?
	going to have	

	We're	having	lamb chops.
		going to have	
Maybe	we'll	have	

FUTURE CONTINUOUS WITH *WILL*

	Will	you they	be	taking	pictures today?
When	will	he she	be	using	the camera?

I He She We They	will ('ll) won't	be	taking	pictures until 3:00.

PRESENT PERFECT

How long	have	you they	worked [t]	at Frank's?
			lived [d]	here?
	has	he she	wanted [əd]	to move?

> The past participle of regular verbs is the same as the past tense form.

I We They	have ('ve) haven't	worked	at Frank's	for three years. since 1982.
		lived	here	
He She	has ('s) hasn't	wanted	to move	

> he's = he is *or* he has
> she's = she is *or* she has

> When the verbs *live, work, study*, and *teach* are used with expressions of duration, there is little difference in meaning between the present perfect and the present perfect continuous.

PRESENT PERFECT CONTINUOUS

| Why | have | I you we they | been | feeling | tired? |
| | Has | he she | been | working | too hard? |

| I You We They | have ('ve) haven't | been | sleeping | enough. |
| He She | has ('s) hasn't | | | |

PAST PERFECT

| | Had | you they | run | in a race before? |
| When | had | he she | been | in a race? |

> past participle

| I He She We They | had ('d) hadn't | run | in this race before. |

PAST PERFECT CONTINUOUS

| | Had | you they | been | living | in Paris then? |
| How long | had | he she | been | living | in Paris? |

| I He She We They | had ('d) hadn't | been | living | in Paris for three years. |

132

The passive

WITH PRESENT TENSE VERBS

Subject	Present tense verb	Object
Factory workers	make	most clothing.
Travel agents	sell	airline tickets.

Subject	Present of *be*	Past participle	Prepositional phrase
Most clothing	is	made	by factory workers.
Airline tickets	are	sold	by travel agents.

agent

WITH PAST TENSE VERBS

Subject	Past tense verb	Object
Tolstoy	wrote	*War and Peace.*
Steven Spielberg	directed	*Jaws* and *E.T.*

Subject	Past of *be*	Past participle	Prepositional phrase
War and Peace	was	written	by Tolstoy.
Jaws and *E.T.*	were	directed	by Steven Spielberg.

> When it is unnecessary to name the agent, it is omitted in passive sentences:
> My son was fired. = "They" fired my son.

WITH PRESENT PERFECT VERBS

Subject	Present perfect verb	Object
They	haven't fixed	my radiator.
We	've notified	the landlord.

Subject	Present perfect of *be*	Past Participle
My radiator	hasn't been	fixed.
The landlord	has been	notified.

WITH PAST PERFECT VERBS

Subject	Past perfect verb	Object
They	had sent	a repair person.
He	hadn't fixed	the radiator.

Subject	Past perfect of *be*	Past participle
A repair person	had been	sent.
The radiator	hadn't been	fixed.

Modal auxiliaries

PRESENT OR FUTURE TIME

Active

Someone	must	fix	the sidewalk.	an obligation
Someone	should	fix	the sidewalk.	a recommendation
The repairs	could would	prevent	an accident.	a result
That big hole	may might	injure	someone. ◄	a possibility
That big hole	must	annoy	people.	a logical conclusion
Someone	can	fix	the sidewalk.	ability
You	may can	file	a complaint.	permission
Someone	will	repair	the sidewalk.	future time

▲ base form

Passive

The sidewalk	must		fixed.
The sidewalk	should		fixed.
An accident	could would		prevented.
Someone	may might	be	injured.
People	must		annoyed.
The sidewalk	can		fixed.
A complaint	may can		filed.
The sidewalk	will		repaired.

▲ past participle

PAST TIME

Active

They	should		arrested	the driver.	a judgment
They	could would	have	prevented	the accident.	a result
The driver	may might		injured	someone. ◄	a possibility
They	must		called	an ambulance.	a logical conclusion

▲ past participle

Passive

The driver	should			arrested.
The accident	could would	have	been	prevented.
Someone	may might			injured.
An ambulance	must			called.

▲ past participle

Conditional sentences

POSSIBLE CONDITIONS

	Present tense form	Future tense
If	I have time (I might),	I'll play tennis.
	I don't have time (I might not),	I won't go to the gym.

CONTRARY-TO-FACT CONDITIONS: PRESENT

	Past tense form	Conditional
If	I had time (I don't),	I'd play tennis.
	I didn't have time (I do),	I wouldn't go to the gym.

I'd = I had *or* I would.

CONTRARY-TO-FACT CONDITIONS: PAST

	Past perfect form	Past conditional
If	I'd had time (I didn't),	I would have played tennis.
	I hadn't had time (I did),	I wouldn't have gone to the gym.

Some irregular verbs

Simple form	Simple past	Past participle	Simple form	Simple past	Past participle
be	was, were	been	lie	lay	lain
become	became	become	lose	lost	lost
begin	began	begun	make	made	made
break	broke	broken	mean	meant	meant
bring	brought	brought	meet	met	met
build	built	built	pay	paid	paid
buy	bought	bought	put	put	put
catch	caught (cot)	caught (cot)	quit	quit	quit
choose	chose	chosen	read [riyd]	read [red]	read [red]
come	came	come	ride	rode	ridden
cost	cost	cost	ring	rang	rung
cut	cut	cut	run	ran	run
do	did	done	say	said	said
draw	drew	drawn	see	saw	seen
drink	drank	drunk	sell	sold	sold
drive	drove	driven	send	sent	sent
eat	ate	eaten	set	set	set
fall	fell	fallen	shoot	shot	shot
feel	felt	felt	shut	shut	shut
fight	fought	fought	sing	sang	sung
find	found	found	sink	sank	sunk
fit	fit	fit	sit	sat	sat
fly	flew	flown	sleep	slept	slept
forget	forgot	forgotten	speak	spoke	spoken
get	got	gotten	spend	spent	spent
give	gave	given	stand	stood	stood
go	went	gone	steal	stole	stolen
grow	grew	grown	swim	swam	swum
have	had	had	take	took	taken
hear	heard (herd)	heard	teach	taught	taught
hide	hid	hidden	tear	tore	torn
hit	hit	hit	tell	told	told
hold	held	held	think	thought	thought
hurt	hurt	hurt	throw	threw	thrown
keep	kept	kept	understand	understood	understood
know	knew	known	wake	woke	woken
lay (ley)	laid	laid	wear	wore	worn
leave	left	left	win	won	won
let	let	let	write	wrote	written

fit (calzar)

lay (

Supplementary Vocabulary

Some countries, nationalities, and languages

Country	Nationality	Major language(s)
Argentina	Argentine	Spanish
Australia	Australian	English
Austria	Austrian	German
Belgium	Belgian	French/Flemish
Bolivia	Bolivian	Spanish
Brazil	Brazilian	Portuguese
Canada	Canadian	English/French
Chile	Chilean	Spanish
China	Chinese	Chinese
Colombia	Colombian	Spanish
Costa Rica	Costa Rican	Spanish
Czechoslovakia	Czechoslovakian	Czech
Denmark	Danish	Danish
the Dominican Republic	Dominican	Spanish
Ecuador	Ecuadorian	Spanish
Egypt	Egyptian	Arabic
Finland	Finnish	Finnish
France	French	French
Germany	German	German
Great Britain	British	English
Guatemala	Guatemalan	Spanish
Greece	Greek	Greek
Haiti	Haitian	Creole/French
The Netherlands	Dutch	Dutch
Hungary	Hungarian	Hungarian
Indonesia	Indonesian	Indonesian
India	Indian	Hindi
Ireland	Irish	English
Israel	Israeli	Hebrew/Arabic
Italy	Italian	Italian
Japan	Japanese	Japanese
Korea	Korean	Korean
Lebanon	Lebanese	Arabic
Mexico	Mexican	Spanish
Norway	Norwegian	Norwegian
Peru	Peruvian	Spanish
Panama	Panamanian	Spanish
Paraguay	Paraguayan	Spanish
Poland	Polish	Polish
Portugal	Portuguese	Portuguese
Saudi Arabia	Saudi	Arabic
Spain	Spanish	Spanish
Sweden	Swedish	Swedish
Switzerland	Swiss	French/German
Thailand	Thai	Thai
Turkey	Turkish	Turkish
the United States	American	English
Uruguay	Uruguayan	Spanish
the U.S.S.R.	Soviet	Russian
Venezuela	Venezuelan	Spanish

Some Sports

- archery
- automobile racing
- badminton
- baseball
- basketball
- bicycle racing
- bowling
- boxing
- canoeing
- dog-sled racing
- fencing
- field hockey
- football
- golf
- handball
- hang gliding
- hiking
- hockey
- horse racing
- ice-skating
- jai alai
- jogging
- judo
- karate
- lacrosse
- mountain climbing
- polo
- racquetball
- roller-skating
- running
- sailing
- scuba diving
- skiing
- skydiving
- soccer
- softball
- squash
- surfing
- swimming
- table tennis
- tennis
- volleyball
- water-skiing
- weightlifting
- wrestling